HEROES OF THE MAJOR LEAGUES

Biographical sketches of ten famous players of the American and National leagues, with exciting accounts of their rise to stardom. Included are Frank Robinson, Brooks Robinson, Roberto Clemente, Hank Aaron, Joe Torre, Sandy Koufax, Juan Marichal, Al Kaline, Harmon Killebrew and Tony Oliva.

HEROES OF THE MAJOR LEAGUES

by Alexander Peters
Illustrated with photographs

Random House • New York

Photograph credits: Joseph Cosentino, © 1966, The Curtis Publishing Co., 146, 157; Malcolm W. Emmons, 79, 128; Ken Regan, Roy Cummings Photo Agency, 2, 20, 36, 58, 74, 92, 110, 136, 143, 160, 162; UPI, 5, 40, 47, 53, 64, 71, 96, 107, 115, 126, 141, 154, 167 (bottom); Wide World, 8, 16, 29, 34, 43, 67, 89, 119, 121, 139, 159, 167 (top), 176; Wally Yost, 76. Cover: Ken Regan, Roy Cummings Photo Agency

This title was originally catalogued by the Library of Congress as follows:

Peters, Alexander.
  Heroes of the major leagues. Illustrated with photos. New York, Random House [1967]
    viii, 184 p. ports. 22 cm. (Little League library, 8)
    CONTENTS. — Frank Robinson. — Roberto Clemente. — Sandy Koufax.—Harmon Killebrew.—Juan Marichal.—Hank Aaron.—Al Kaline.—Tony Oliva.—Joe Torre.—Brooks Robinson.

  1. Baseball—Juvenile literature.   I. Title.
GV873.P42   j 920   67–5680

Trade Ed.: ISBN: 0- **394-80188-1**   Lib. Ed.: ISBN: 0-394-90188-6

© Copyright, 1967, by Random House, Inc.
All rights reserved under International and Pan-American Copyright Conventions. Published in New York by Random House, Inc., and simultaneously in Toronto, Canada, by Random House of Canada Limited.

Manufactured in the United States of America

Printed by The Colonial Press, Clinton, Mass.

CONTENTS

What's a Hero?	vii
1. Frank Robinson	3
2. Roberto Clemente	21
3. Sandy Koufax	37
4. Harmon Killebrew	59
5. Juan Marichal	77
6. Hank Aaron	93
7. Al Kaline	111
8. Tony Oliva	129
9. Joe Torre	147
10. Brooks Robinson	163
Index	179

What's a Hero?

There is no formula descripton for a hero—not even for a major league baseball hero. They come in all shapes and sizes and from all walks of life. The line-up of *Heroes of the Major Leagues* includes ten current baseball players who unquestionably are heroes to many thousands of sports fans of all ages, and no two of them are exactly alike.

If there is a single theme that seems to be common to every one of them, it is the fact that none became an "instant" or "overnight" star. They climbed slowly to the top of their profession through consistent and often spectacular performances at bat, on the mound or in the field. They experienced disappointments and handicaps that would have overcome weaker men.

The baseball world did not truly accept Frank Robinson as a hero until he was traded by the

Reds to the Orioles in 1966 and then won every honor in sight, including the world championship for his team.

Sandy Koufax was once one of the wildest pitchers in baseball. Juan Marichal started out as a shortstop in the Dominican Republic; when he came to the United States he had difficulty in adjusting to its language and customs. Both Puerto Rican-born Roberto Clemente and Cuban-born Tony Oliva experienced many of the same problems.

Harmon Killebrew has won many American League home-run titles, but early in his career he had to endure the remark of a manager who said, "He throws like a girl."

As a youngster, Joe Torre was fat and Al Kaline suffered from a bone disease. Brooks Robinson, both as a boy and a big leaguer, has had to cope with injuries that would have permanently sidelined a less determined athlete.

Most youthful baseball players dream that one day they will become big leaguers. Few ever make it, of course, but these stories prove that a player can be underrated, fat, prone to injuries, born in a foreign country, or wild on the mound and still reach the magic land reserved for the heroes of baseball.

HEROES OF THE MAJOR LEAGUES

Frank Robinson 1

Tall, broad-shouldered Don Drysdale of the Los Angeles Dodgers scowled at the batter, Frank Robinson. It was the first tense moment of the 1966 World Series. Drysdale peered briefly at one of Robinson's Baltimore Oriole teammates, inching off first base. Then he flung a fast ball.

Robinson whipped his bat into the shoulder-high pitch. With a low moan, the stunned Dodger Stadium crowd of 55,941 watched the ball sail high and far into the left-field grandstand for a home run. It was only the first inning of the Series and already the underdog Orioles led the Dodgers, 2–0.

"I was kind of looking for that pitch," Robinson told delighted teammates in the dugout.

Then Oriole teammate Brooks Robinson promptly put another Drysdale pitch into the seats. The Dodgers never did gain the lead—in that game or the three that followed. And in the fourth game, at Baltimore's Memorial Stadium, Frank Robinson defiantly crowded the plate against the powerful Drysdale again. The slim, right-handed hitter leaned over, his left elbow jutting into the path Drysdale's pitch would take. The 210-pound hurler fired, Robinson lashed out and the ball rocketed into the stands for another homer.

It proved to be the only run of the game, and it clinched the world championship for the Orioles. Robinson was voted the outstanding player of the Series. In the clubhouse afterward, teammates nodded knowingly when he told sports writers, "This has been my most satisfying season. But it's been a long one. It started for me last December ninth."

That was the day Robinson was traded to the Orioles for three players by the Cincinnati Reds of the National League. Robinson had played 10 fine seasons for the Reds, and he held most of their all-time batting records. At $50,000, he was the highest-paid player in the team's history. In addition,

Frank Robinson heads for first base after hitting a homer off Dodger Don Drysdale in the fourth game of the 1966 Series.

the hard-hitting outfielder held a lifetime batting average of .303. News of the trade shocked him. It also amazed players in both leagues, and fans all over the United States. If ever an athlete was on trial when he reported to a new team, 30-year-old Frank Robinson was that athlete. But no big leaguer ever responded more strongly.

Robinson arrived late in the Orioles' training camp after moving his wife and two children from Cincinnati. Teammates watched intently the first time Manager Hank Bauer asked him to pinch-hit in an intra-squad game. Then they grinned. Robinson walloped a line drive off the left-field fence at Miami Stadium.

When the Orioles played their first spring exhibition against major league opposition, Robinson—wearing the same number 20 that he had worn at Cincinnati—started them off with a homer.

In Boston's Fenway Park on April 12, in the Orioles' American League opening game, Robinson scored the first run, clubbed a homer and helped his new team to a 5–4 victory in extra innings.

Few rivals forget their first impressions of Robinson. His new teammates were equally impressed. During Frank's first visit to New York's Yankee Stadium, the thin-legged outfielder tore up part of the baseline while sliding safely into the bag, head first. Manager Bauer gestured toward several of his other players and chuckled. "They'll probably all try that now. They usually follow what he does. This is our eighth game, and that's about the eighth time he's taken a base where practically nobody else would try."

Another night at Yankee Stadium, Robinson slammed into the concrete right-field wall, then flipped over backward into the seats to make a spectacular, run-saving catch. As the season went on, the Orioles' first-place lead grew. Robinson acted the role of daredevil less often. Some people recalled a remark that a Cincinnati teammate had once made: "You'll seldom see Frank steal a base when the team is five or six runs ahead. It's the 2-to-1 game when he steals or takes an extra base. Everybody knows he's a good hitter, but I never saw a base runner with greater instincts. Faster, yes. But better, no."

From the flying start supplied by Frank and Brooks Robinson, the Orioles sped to such a huge lead that rivals all but gave up their pennant hopes by mid-July. In September, when the Orioles clinched their first American League title, Hank Bauer summed up the season neatly. "There's no

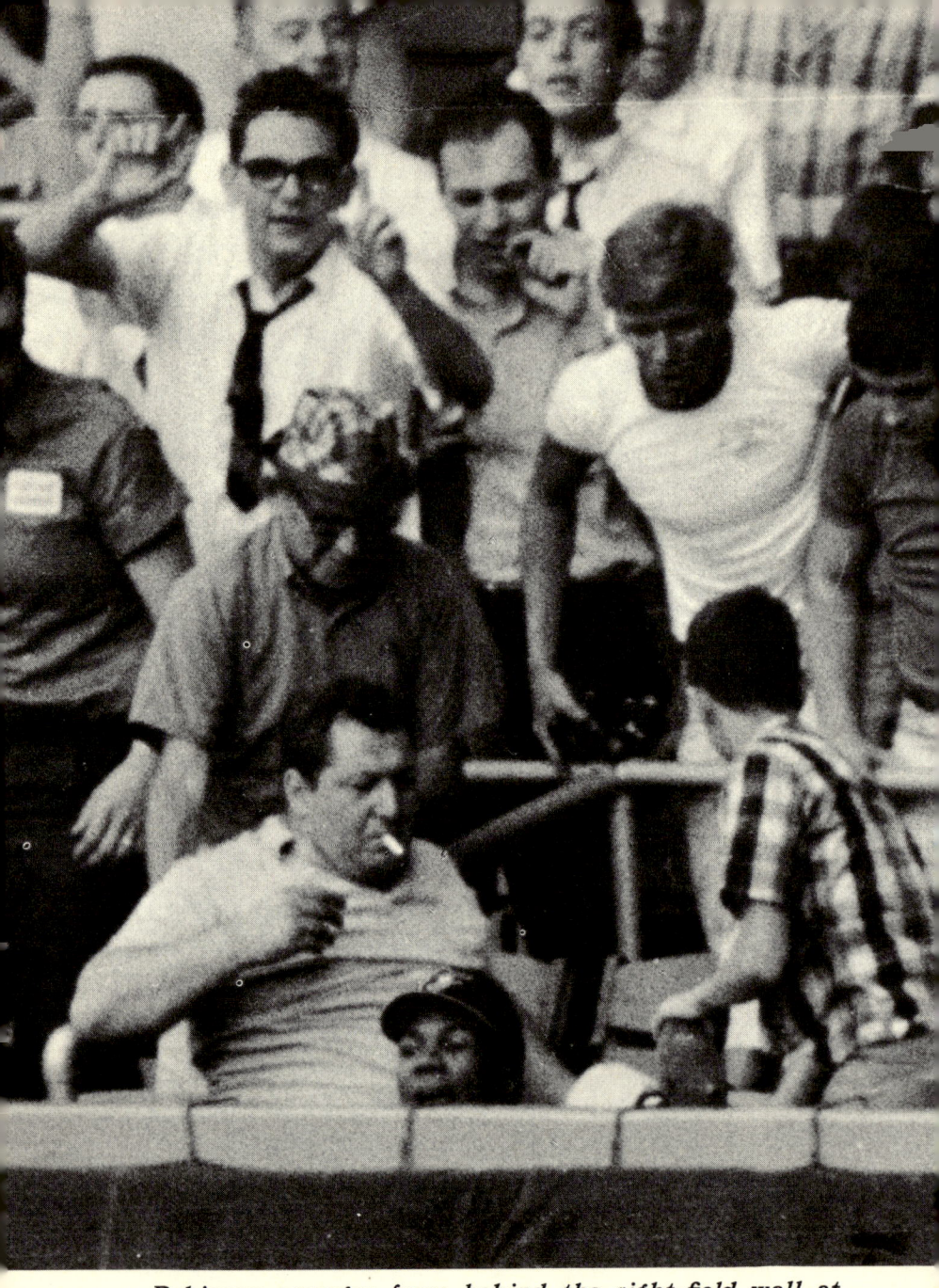

Robinson emerges from behind the right-field wall at Yankee Stadium after making an almost impossible run-saving catch.

doubt Frank was the big guy."

Robinson became the twelfth major leaguer to win the Triple Crown. He led in batting with .316, in runs-batted-in with 122 and in home runs with 49. But there was more to his value. As Harry Dalton, the Orioles' director of personnel, put it: "We looked at the statistics, of course, when we made the trade for Robinson. But you don't realize how much he really helps until you get him in your uniform. Then you see. He's always helping the younger players with their hitting, and he's a great needler. He keeps the team laughing, and he's always alive, even on the bench."

Robinson's Triple Crown was the first in the American League since Mickey Mantle of the New York Yankees had won it ten years earlier. But superstar Mantle was no more than a name to Frank Robinson in 1956. That year the slender, strong-armed Negro was thinking only about winning a job with the Cincinnati Reds, and playing in the National League. Even that looked like a tough job.

The Reds scouted Robinson while he was playing American Legion baseball. He starred in baseball and basketball for McClymonds High School in Oakland, California, where his family had moved from Beaumont, Texas, when Frank was only four. There were 10 other children in the family, but as soon as he grew old enough to play baseball, Frank saw less and less of his brothers and sisters. In the summer he spent most of his time playing ball. If he got home for dinner at all, he got there late. "I can't remember having a hot meal from the time I was 12 until I signed with the Reds," he once said.

It was no wonder. Even after the Oakland parks closed for the night, the local community center provided a place to play the game indoors. Gene Powles, the Cincinnati scout who first spotted Robinson, recalls him as a shy, skinny youngster who played every game as if it were his last. "Do some pushups. Work on those muscles," Powles advised Frank. "You've got to build up your shoulders and wrists."

That was all the instruction the eager youngster needed. "That boy shook the house down doing those silly exercises," his mother remembers.

Frank was 17 when the Reds signed him for a bonus of $3,000. In the next two years he hit 42 home runs and batted .348, then .336 for the Reds' farm clubs. But 1955, his third year in the minors, was a bad one. Robinson had arm trouble. His throwing suffered so much that he was shifted from the outfield to first base. He slipped to a total of 12 homers and hit only .263 at Columbia, South Carolina. Several Cincinnati officials doubted he could make the jump to the majors.

"Don't worry," they were advised by Manager George "Birdie" Tebbetts, who had seen Robinson play when Frank was healthy and strong. "If that kid can throw from left field to second base," said Tebbetts, "he'll be my left fielder. Do you know that Robinson can stop his swing right in the middle of the plate? Ted Williams is one of the few others I've ever seen who could do that."

Another tribute to Frank's natural batting ability came from the veteran coach and manager, Jimmie Dykes. "He's so quick with his wrists," Dykes said, "that he can literally hit a ball out of the catcher's glove."

Robinson met his first big challenge solidly. Fully recovered, he played 152 games for the Reds in 1956 and smashed 38 homers. Cincinnati tied a major league record with 221 four-baggers. Led by rookie Robinson, the Reds' outfield—the other players were Wally Post and Gus Bell—became the first to smack more than 100 homers in a season. The baseball writers named Robinson Rookie of the Year.

The 1957 season went just as well. The 195-pound

slugger hit .322 and earned Sophomore of the Year honors. He seemed on the road to early stardom. Then, during a Florida exhibition game in the spring of 1958, something happened to halt his progress. In fact, it threatened his career.

Leaning forward in his regular batting stance, dangerously close to the plate, Robinson was clipped on the head by a pitch. When he finally got back into the line-up, he found himself moving his feet, pulling away from pitches. For the first half of the year pitchers kept fooling him. He couldn't raise his average over .250.

"I kept telling myself I wasn't afraid," Robinson recalled later. "But I still couldn't keep from rolling back on my heels every time a pitcher curved me. Then all of a sudden, I wasn't falling back any more. I guess I got so mad at myself I didn't care what happened."

By the time the season ended, Robinson had lifted his average to .269. He had proved something to himself. But his all-out, reckless play did something else, too. It convinced rival players that the Cincinnati speedster didn't care whom he hurt—himself or others. He became known in the big leagues as an angry young man. As long as he stayed in the National League, some part of that label clung to Frank Robinson.

Veteran infielder Eddie Kasko once admitted at Cincinnati: "Before coming to the Reds, I played two years against Robinson and I hated him. He challenges you all the time." And one of the best pitchers of the era, Robin Roberts of the Philadelphia Phils, found Frank anything but friendly. "There's something about the way he stands at the plate," Roberts said. "He sort of bristles. He wants to hurt you. And he usually does."

It was a kind of grudging respect. Robinson recognized that. However, charges that he slid too hard and too high bothered him. But he didn't try to deny them. He retorted hotly, "Baseball isn't a popularity contest. I'm not here to win friends, just ball games."

Robinson proved his point one sultry day in 1960. He tore into third base so hard that he bowled over Eddie Mathews, the muscular third baseman of the Milwaukee Braves. Mathews came up swinging. Before umpires could stop the fight, Robinson landed several punches. Mathews did not fail to connect, either. The Cincinnati trainer wiped the blood off Robinson's lumpy face. He patched and swabbed the cuts. Then, with his left eye so puffed up that it was almost shut, Robinson ran back onto the field for the second game of the double-header.

Mathews was not the only player who was surprised when Robinson socked a two-run homer and a double. But he was the most unhappy. Then Robinson moved out onto the field where he topped off his performance with a diving catch that robbed Mathews of an extra-base hit. Shaking his head in admiration, Mathews admitted, "That's the best way to get even."

Robinson's restless moods bothered Cincinnati players, too. But many of them did not realize that he was lonely. Until the arrival in 1959 of another Oakland boy, outfielder Vada Pinson, perhaps Robinson himself did not realize how deep his loneliness had grown. "I used to brood when I didn't play well," he admitted much later in his career. "Now I brood only when I'm not helping the team."

By 1961 Robinson had begun noticeably to change. He was quieter and more mature when he reported to camp that spring. The fire still burned within him, but he kept it burning low. Teammates saw it flash occasionally. There was the time when the Reds, playing poorly, lost three straight games to the Chicago Cubs. Robinson called a clubhouse meeting and woke them up with a stinging lecture.

There was also a feud with Dodger pitcher Drysdale. During one game the powerful right-hander brushed back Robinson from the plate twice. But Robinson stepped back up and dug his cleats into the same spot in the batter's box. Drysdale delivered again—on a count of three balls, no strikes —and whacked Robinson painfully on the elbow.

Quietly furious, Robinson trotted down to first base. But he didn't take his revenge until a few weeks later. In a double-header against the Dodgers, he slammed two homers, a double and a single, driving home seven Cincinnati runs. The Reds won both games. No teammate could doubt Robinson's wisdom when he said afterward, "The best way to retaliate is with a base hit." He had proved it in two different seasons—first against Mathews and the Braves in 1960, now against Drysdale and the Dodgers.

The Reds of 1961 won the pennant by four games, giving Cincinnati its first league title in 21 years. Robinson was also named Most Valuable Player in the National League. He matched this honor five years later in the American League, something no other player has done. A month after the 1961 season ended, Robinson married Barbara Ann Cole.

Beaned by a close Dodger pitch, Frank is helped to his feet by a Cincinnati teammate.

It was a happy end to a happy year.

However, both Robinson and the team lost their titles in 1962. The leader of the Reds had another excellent season, however. He boosted his home-run total from 37 to 39, his RBI total from 124 to 136 and his batting average from .323 to .342.

At the end of that season, Robinson threatened to quit baseball. Sports writers scoffed. They claimed he was merely trying to get a salary hike from the Reds' president and general manager, William DeWitt. Teammates laughed and handed him a gag present wrapped in gift paper: a lunch pail. But the Reds' front office did give Robinson a raise, a big one.

Was he actually serious about quitting? "I honestly meant it at the time," Robinson insists. Yet he continued to call the 1962 season his finest in baseball—until the remarkable trade with the Orioles.

The Reds were in the 1965 pennant race most of the way. But they flopped late in the season and one of the casualties was their popular manager, Dick Sisler. He was fired by DeWitt. As for Robinson, he had anything but a great year. For the average player, it would have been wonderful: 33 homers, 113 RBIs, and a .296 batting average. But Robinson was a highly paid star. Two months after the end of the season, DeWitt dropped his bombshell. Robinson had been traded to Baltimore for two pitchers and an outfielder.

"I was a lot more surprised when they let Frank go than when they dropped me," said the astonished Sisler. "He was a leader. You don't replace that kind that easily."

Robinson didn't deny his indignation over being traded to another team. "I didn't want to leave my friends," he said. "But the trade gave me a little extra incentive. I had to prove them wrong. I had to prove myself."

At least DeWitt had been smart enough to send Robinson to another league. Those who provoked Frank's anger, National League rivals knew, were in peril. The brush-back pitch is part of almost every hurler's collection, and Robinson is a natural target for the brush-back with his close-to-the-plate stance. In his 11 major league seasons, he has been hit by pitches 128 times. Yet Manager Gene Mauch of the Philadelphia Phils feared Robinson's revenge so much that he made a rule for his pitchers: Don't throw knockdown pitches to Frank Robinson. "That man is trouble enough any time," reasoned Mauch. "Get him riled and you've just got more trouble."

Drysdale and the Dodgers had learned the lesson long before the 1966 World Series. Los Angeles left-hander Ron Perranoski, one of the game's finest relief pitchers, pointed out: "Robinson is a great hitter. He hangs over the plate, but there's no way to drive him away. If you knock him down three straight times, he'll get up and hit the ball over the wall. That just makes him madder. I've seen it."

Fans in Baltimore will never forget Frank Robinson's 1966 season. Only Robinson himself knows if he was still, in any way, an angry man. The citizens of Baltimore think not. They saw how well he rose to the occasion.

As a reminder of one of Robinson's most noteworthy feats of the season, a small pennant flutters along the top row of seats in Memorial Stadium. It marks the spot where he almost put a home-run ball into orbit. In a game against the Cleveland Indians, he became the first batter to knock a ball all the way out of the Birds' huge stadium—a blow later measured at an incredible 579 feet. The little flag was inscribed simply: "Here." Not another word was needed.

Roberto Clemente 2

To some sports fans it might appear that 1966 was a disappointing year for Roberto Clemente. He was striving for his third straight National League batting title and he failed to make it. In addition, his team—the Pittsburgh Pirates—were in the thick of the pennant race and they did not make it either. But despite the failures, 1966 was the best season Roberto had ever had in his 12 years with the Pirates. It was the season when he was finally appreciated.

Clemente, a man of great pride, had been disturbed for years by a lack of recognition. The 1960 season especially annoyed him. That year the Pirates won the pennant and the World Series and Roberto, an emerging superstar, had his best season up to that time. He hit .314 and batted in 94 runs. Teammate Dick Groat, on the other hand, led the league with a .325 batting average, though he batted in only 50 runs. However, there was no doubt that Groat, the fiery shortstop, was the team's inspirational leader. In the voting for the league's Most Valuable Player, Groat won.

"I should have won," said Clemente a couple of years later. "I carried the club all year."

He also did well enough in the World Series—much better than the New York Yankees expected. They took one look at this free-swinging hitter and could hardly wait to pitch to him. But Clemente's appearance was deceiving. He got at least one hit in each of the seven games and finished with a .310 Series average. Even so, as Roberto recalls it today, "The only way you could find my name in the papers was with a magnifying glass."

It is not surprising that when the Series ended with a dramatic Pittsburgh home run in the last inning of the seventh game, Roberto hustled out of the jubilant atmosphere of the clubhouse and flew home to Puerto Rico. In fact, today he wears his 1961 All-Star Game ring instead of his 1960 World Series ring. He prefers to remember the game in which he batted in Willie Mays twice. The second hit was in the tenth inning and chalked up the winning National League run.

It would be easy to draw from this a picture of a selfish ballplayer. But it would be a false picture of Roberto Clemente. Clemente is the essence of the team man and truly happy only when the team is doing well. No one, for example, was more excited than Roberto after the Pirates clinched the 1960 pennant.

He stood in the batter's box while the public-address announcer told the crowd that the Cubs had beaten the Cardinals, making the Pirates the league champions. Overjoyed, Clemente hit a single off Warren Spahn. Then, when teammate Hal Smith doubled, Roberto ignored the third-base coach's signal to hold up. Instead he slid into home on his belly.

"Stop at third?" he said later. "I wanted to get to the bench quick, and talk about winning the pennant."

Roberto's enthusiasm shows itself off the field too. When he isn't playing ball, he spends a great deal of time with children. In Puerto Rico he is in-

in a program to combat juvenile delinquency. And in the United States he visits children in hospitals, making all the arrangements himself and refusing to let photographers accompany him. "I do not go because the club wants me to go," he says. "I go because *I* want to go."

Roberto was born in Carolina, Puerto Rico, on August 18, 1934. It was the height of the Depression, but he has only pleasant memories of his childhood. His father was the foreman of a sugar plantation and owned some trucks which he hired out for shipping jobs. Although Roberto's parents were not wealthy, they were able to give their six children proper food and clothing. Even more important, they taught Roberto what it means to belong to a large family whose members love one another.

"I never heard any hate in my house," Clemente has said. "Not for anybody. I never heard my mother say a bad word to my father, or my father to my mother. During the war, when food all over Puerto Rico was limited, we never went hungry. They always found a way to feed us. We kids were first, and they were second."

Roberto proved to be a grateful son. Shortly after he joined the Pirates in 1955, he bought his parents a home in Puerto Rico. "I do not think I am giving my parents something," he said. "I am trying to pay them back for giving me so much."

As a boy Roberto displayed many talents. He played baseball well, of course, but he was also good at track. In high school he threw the javelin 195 feet, high-jumped 6 feet and triple-jumped 45. It seemed possible that he might be a member of the 1956 United States Olympic Team. Roberto also did well in his studies and wanted to study engineering at a university in Puerto Rico.

Baseball, however, interrupted all of his plans. When Roberto was 17, he signed a contract for a $500 bonus and $60 a month to play in the Puerto Rican league. He did so well that, by his senior year of high school, nine major league teams were interested in him. The Dodgers offered him a $6,000 bonus—one of the largest bonuses ever offered a Latin American ballplayer. Roberto said yes, and then later that day received a $40,000 offer from Milwaukee, an unheard-of sum in Puerto Rico.

Roberto went home and told his mother his problem. But to Mrs. Clemente there was no problem. "If you give your word," she said, "you keep your word." Roberto signed with the Dodgers.

The Dodgers sent Clemente to Montreal, where he hit .257 in 87 games. Because of the bonus rule that year, the Dodgers could not protect him in the annual major league player draft and Pittsburgh grabbed him. What was Roberto's reaction? "I did not even know where Pittsburgh was," he says.

Clemente's rookie year, 1955, was not pleasant. He had to overcome his tendency to swing at bad balls and bob his head when he swung. But as bad as life was on the field, it was even worse off the field. He could not speak English very well and he had difficulty in adjusting to a new way of life.

"Latin Americans lead different lives in the United States," he says. "We are always meeting new people, seeing new faces. Everything is strange. We have trouble ordering food in restaurants. And you have no idea how segregation held some of us back. We Latins are people of high emotions, and coming to this country we need time to settle down emotionally. Once we are relaxed and have no problems, we can play baseball well."

Clemente's adjustment to his new country has been a slow but sure process. He has worked very hard for the recognition he feels he deserves. Unlike Willie Mays and Mickey Mantle his name did not become a household word as soon as he came into the majors. Nor did he achieve their almost immediate success. But as he grew more relaxed, and his problems became fewer and fewer, he played better baseball. There were hints of greatness in his first five seasons (1955–1959).

When Clemente finally did emerge from his relative obscurity in 1960, the fans particularly noticed his resemblance to Mays. Playing right field with flash and dash, Roberto sometimes ran out from under his cap, chasing line drives and making basket catches. His throwing arm was so strong and accurate that opponents could not take chances. At bat, he hit solidly and viciously. And on the bases he turned singles into doubles.

"Willie is a very good ballplayer," said Clemente, "but why does everybody say I run like Willie, catch like Willie, throw like Willie and hit line drives like Willie? I am not Willie. I am Roberto Clemente. That means I play only like Roberto Clemente. Many people tell me I want to play like Willie. From little boy up I always play like this. I always want to run fast, to throw long and hit far."

In 1961 Clemente showed people he had a style all his own and thereafter people did not compare him to Mays quite as much. He won his first batting title with a .351 average—higher than Mays had ever hit. Clemente also showed his power for the first time. He hit 23 home runs—only three less than in his first five seasons put together.

Roberto hit .312 and .320 during the next two seasons and then won his second and third batting titles in 1964 and 1965 with averages of .339 and .329. From 1960 through 1966 his batting average was never less than .312. He established himself as the most consistent hitter in the major leagues.

Despite all this, Clemente was still having difficulties. Though he had finally become a favorite of the fans, he was having trouble with his managers. The managers thought that Clemente was too concerned about his health. He has frequently been accused of being a hypochondriac. For a long time after he came into the majors he complained of a bad back. He said that he had injured it by swinging too hard while playing in the Puerto Rican League in 1953.

In 1954 his back was injured again in an auto accident. Clemente had just visited his brother, who was dying of a brain tumor. While he was driving home, a drunken driver smashed into him at 60 miles an hour. Three of Roberto's spinal discs were jarred loose. His back did not get better until three years later.

An enthusiastic Clemente knocks his opponents' catcher off balance as he slides safely home.

He had other injuries, too. While throwing sidearm one day in 1958, he cracked his right elbow. Three years later, a pitch from Don Drysdale hit him on the same elbow and he had to undergo surgery to remove a bone chip. It is impossible to deny the importance of injuries like that, but Roberto complained so often about minor ailments that some people thought perhaps he was just imagining things. He constantly seemed to be having colds, flu attacks or a nervous stomach.

The problem reached a peak in 1963. "The Pittsburgh press had me at odds with Danny Murtaugh [the Pirates manager]. They never said it exactly that way, but they knew how to say it other ways," Clemente has said. "I caught the flu in San Francisco. Then we flew to Los Angeles, and we had shrimp and steak on the plane. I got sick in my room at three A.M. I began to sweat. I had the shakes. I called the doctor at six. His nurse told me to put hot towels on my stomach. Later that morning they pumped out my stomach. I went to the ball park and Murtaugh asked me how I felt."

Clemente told him he felt terrible, but the manager said he was to play anyway. During the game Roberto struck out twice and got one hit.

The next day Clemente complained of feeling

dizzy. Then Murtaugh really laid it on the line. "I think you're the best in the league," he told Roberto. "You make good money, but you have to put out."

When Roberto insisted he couldn't play, Murtaugh walked away in disgust. Clemente sat out the next three games and the Pittsburgh papers hinted that Murtaugh was "tired" of Clemente's attitude. But Roberto just couldn't understand why people would not believe him, why they insisted on calling it an act. "When I said I had back trouble," he protested, "they call me, 'Mama's Boy.' 'Goldbrick.' When my elbow was swollen big as a softball, they say it was in my head. If I am sick, I do not deny it. If my back is hurting me and I am forced to punch at the ball with no power, I tell the truth."

After the 1963 season, Murtaugh resigned because of his own ill health, and Harry Walker replaced him. At first Clemente had trouble with Walker, too. He injured himself again while mowing his lawn back home in Puerto Rico after the 1964 season. The mower struck a sharp rock, which flew up against Clemente's right thigh. For days his leg pained him, but Roberto refused to stay off it. He was the player-manager for a team in the Puerto

Rican winter baseball league and he wanted to help San Juan win the pennant. But in the league's All-Star game, while he was trotting slowly to first base, his leg buckled. He had popped a ligament. Worse than that, the leg began to swell steadily over the next three days. Taking no chances, Clemente's doctor operated to remove the excess blood that had accumulated.

Clemente failed to report to spring training on time, but not because of his leg. He was in the hospital with a malarial fever which he had picked up at the hog farm he operates. When he finally reported to camp, he was very weak and had lost 25 pounds. During the first month of the season Clemente still wasn't at full strength. Though he was playing, he made it clear to Walker that he needed more rest. At that point, he and Walker reportedly had an argument. Later, Clemente told a Pittsburgh columnist that he wanted to be traded because he could not play for Walker anymore.

After the story broke, Walker and Clemente got together once more and made a determined effort to understand each other. The discussions seemed to work. Clemente was happy again and won his third batting title to prove it.

Getting along with his manager was very important to Clemente. Throughout the 1966 season he liked to tell anyone who would listen how much he enjoyed playing for Walker. "I have more respect for this man than any of my previous managers," said Roberto. "This fellow makes me feel that he really appreciates what I do. When he has something to tell you he tells you in front of everybody. You don't hear about it from some newspaperman."

Clemente was truly giving Walker something to be appreciative about. He had taken over as the undisputed team leader, even though his batting average was only the club's third best. His average slid slightly to .317, but his 29 home runs and 119 runs-batted-in were personal highs.

In addition to his hitting, his spectacular fielding and his inspired base running, Clemente has something else that makes him valuable to the Pirates— he gives his teammates the feeling that they can always count on him for the big hit. A Philadelphia ballplayer put his finger on the quality of Roberto's 1966 performance when he said: "A couple of times a year he used to relax on you. Not this year."

From the Pirates' viewpoint, Manager Walker summed up the situation perfectly at the end of the season when he said, "There's no question about it, Clemente has been the guts of this club. If he's

After winning his first National League batting title in 1961, Roberto poses proudly with Dick Groat (right), the previous year's champion.

not the National League's Most Valuable Player, I'm nuts." The baseball writers of America subsequently proved Walker's sanity when they elected Roberto MVP. It was about time.

Sandy Koufax 3

It was the fifth inning in the final game of the 1966 season, and Sandy Koufax was pitching to Gary Sutherland of the Philadelphia Phillies. The Dodgers were struggling to avoid a play-off with the San Francisco Giants for the pennant. With only two days' rest Sandy had been given the pitching assignment after Don Drysdale had lost to the Phils in the opener of a double-header.

As he followed through on an overhand fast ball, Koufax felt something pop in his left shoulder at the base of the neck. He had frequently felt pain before when pitching, so he did not panic at this new twinge. It was just something more he would have to cope with.

But first he had to dispose of the Phillies. He got Sutherland on a fly ball to left field and retired the side without incident. As soon as Koufax reached the Dodger dugout, he went through the runway under the stands leading to the clubhouse. There he stretched out on a table while Dodger trainers Wayne Anderson and Bill Buhler examined his shoulder. A vertebra had slipped out of place.

"Don't worry," Buhler assured him. "We'll have you back there in no time," and his fingers began probing the afflicted area. By the time the Dodgers went out on the field in the sixth, Sandy had rejoined them. For the next three innings he continued to rely on his fast ball and the Dodgers built up a 6–0 lead.

Now it was the last of the ninth and Sandy needed only three more outs to nail down the pennant. Up to this point, he had allowed only three infield singgles and a double. Richie Allen was first man up for the Phillies in the ninth, and he hit a ground ball that second baseman Jim Lefebvre bobbled for an error. Harvey Kuenn hit a single. Then Tony Taylor singled and Bill White doubled off the scoreboard. Suddenly it was a 6–3 ball game with nobody out.

While Sandy hung his head and stared at the dirt on the pitcher's mound, Walt Alston came striding out of the dugout, calling for time. Koufax hoped the manager wasn't coming to yank him out. But Alston, when he reached the mound, spoke in a calm, collected voice. "Look," he said, "you're throwing only fast balls. You've got to throw some breaking stuff, even if you only show it to them."

Koufax nodded and a moment later he was alone again on the mound, facing the next hitter, Bob Uecker. Sandy mixed in a few curves with his fast ball and struck out Uecker. Bobby Wine was next. Koufax looked back at White on second base, then fired to the plate. Wine hit a grounder to short and Maury Wills played it professionally across the diamond to first base for the second out. Now it was Jackie Brandt's turn. Sandy was at the end of his endurance and wanted to get Brandt out as fast as possible. He quickly put two strikes over the plate. With his remaining strength, he fired a fast ball past Brandt to make him his tenth strikeout victim of the game. The Dodgers had won another pennant on Sandy's fabled left arm.

Inside the Dodger clubhouse, while his teammates celebrated, Sandy sat in a chair. His left arm was wrapped in a rubber sleeve cut from an inner tube

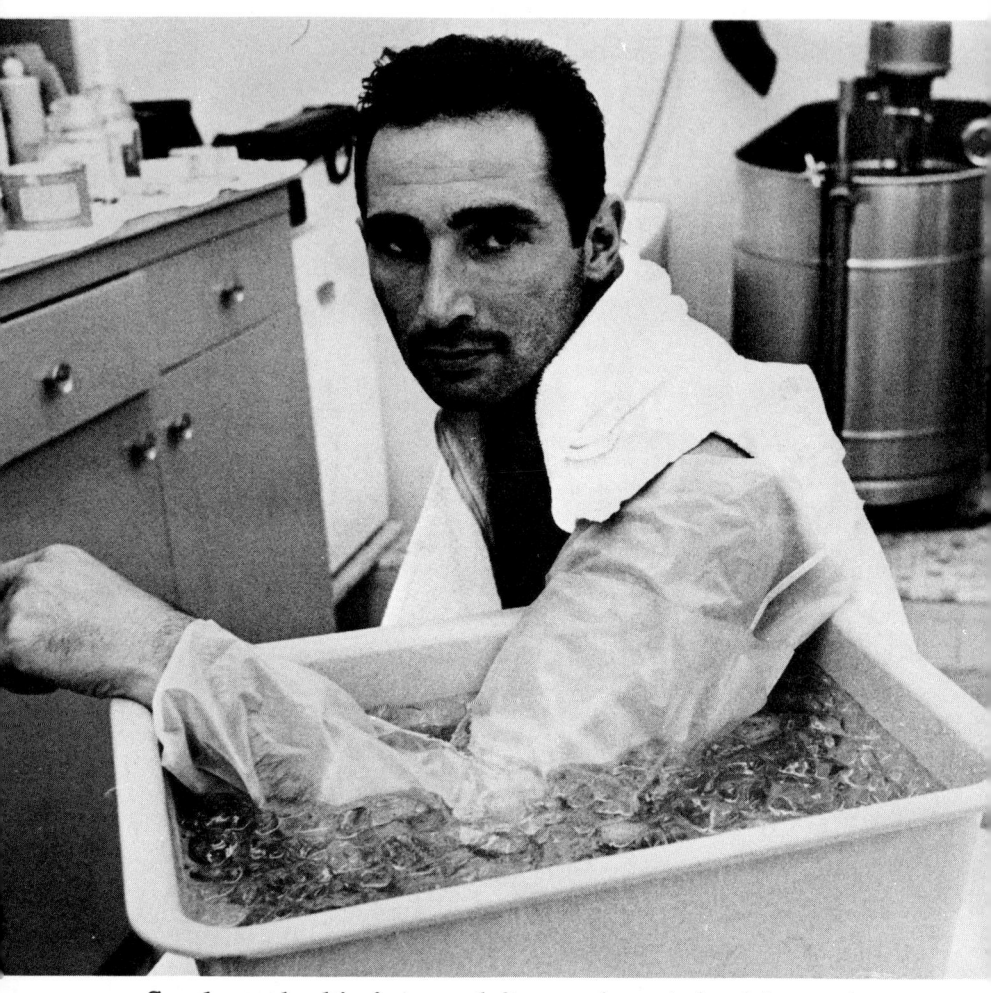
Sandy soaks his famous left arm in a tub of ice water after racking up another victory for the Dodgers.

and immersed in a bucket of ice water.

"Does it hurt?" someone asked, trying to be heard over the din. A grin creased the handsome face still stained with sweat, giving the visitor his answer. It hurt all right, but not as much as losing the ball game would have hurt.

A quick review of the 1966 season will indicate just how much Koufax has achieved. With a record of 27–9 he won more games than any other pitcher in the major leagues. He also pitched more innings (323) and more complete games (27) and struck out more batters (317) than any other pitcher in either league. In fact, he became the first pitcher in baseball history to strike out more than 300 men in three different seasons. In addition, no other National League left-hander in this century has won as many as 27 games in one year. The statistics show that Sandy Koufax is undoubtedly one of the greatest left-handers in the recorded history of the game.

Sandy Koufax was born in Brooklyn, New York, on December 30, 1935. Brooklyn was then the home of the Dodgers, and they were practically a way of life to Brooklyn residents. There were no fans as enthusiastic as Brooklyn's Dodger fans. But as Sandy grew up, baseball and the attraction of the Dodgers made considerably less impression on him than basketball. The Borough of Brooklyn is not abundant with sandlots. It is landscaped with asphalt and concrete basketball courts, and basketball dominated his interest. At Lafayette High School he was a steady scorer and good rebounder, as well as a non-hitting first baseman. In his senior year he earned a basketball scholarship to the University of Cincinnati, where he decided to study architecture.

Up to that point the only baseball he had played had been in his senior year at Lafayette, except for some sandlot ball with a Coney Island team called the Parkviews. The manager of the Parkviews, a man named Milt Laurie, saw the power in Sandy's arm and recommended that he switch from first base to pitching. He also contacted a sports writer for the *Brooklyn Eagle,* Jimmy Murphy, whose beat was schoolboy sports. Laurie told Murphy that he had a player who really could throw a baseball through a brick wall. Murphy came out to watch whenever Sandy pitched.

In his freshman year at Cincinnati, Sandy averaged 10 points a game on the basketball team. In the spring he pitched for the freshman baseball team and struck out 51 batters in 32 innings. When he came back to Brooklyn for the spring holidays, he

Young Koufax as a budding pitching star at the University of Cincinnati.

was given a tryout by the New York Giants (who had not yet moved to San Francisco). The Giants were impressed with his speed, but not his control. They never called him back.

Meanwhile, Murphy was praising Koufax to Al Campanis, a Dodger scout. In September, before Sandy was due to return to Cincinnati for the fall semester, Campanis arranged for a tryout at Brooklyn's Ebbets Field. It was a wet, misty day and the Dodgers skipped batting practice. There were only a few people in the stands. Sandy suited up and came onto the field, where he was joined by Campanis, Walt Alston, Vice President Fresco Thompson and Rube Walker, a second-string catcher. Sandy was 18 years old, and nervous.

"All right," Campanis began. "Try a few fast balls first."

For the next 15 minutes, Sandy pumped fast balls into Rube Walker's mitt. Maybe it was the overcast and damp day or maybe it was the nearly empty ballpark, but every time Sandy released the baseball it seemed to explode in Walker's glove. Presently Campanis called for some curves. Sandy's curve was scarcely the masterful weapon it is today, but he could already put more than a wrinkle on it. The Dodgers, however, weren't really too concerned about his curve—or his control. A promising young pitcher can learn to control his pitches and to throw a variety of curves, but he has to be born with speed. The Dodgers were also especially eager to find out how long Sandy could go on throwing hard before he got tired.

After an hour, the workout was over. The four men went into conference, leaving Sandy by himself.

"What do you think?" Campanis asked Walker.

"You're crazy if you let him get out of the park without signing him," Walker replied.

The Dodgers did let Koufax leave the park without signing him up, but shortly afterward they gave him a contract with a $14,000 bonus. They were paying a considerable amount of money for a pitcher of such limited experience. On the other hand, Sandy was taking a calculated gamble, too. He was giving up his college scholarship and his preparations to become an architect in exchange for the uncertain life of a ballplayer.

Life could not have been more uncertain than it was at the outset of Sandy's first spring at the Dodgers' training camp in 1955. He was just 20 years old and had had no professional experience. He was understandably nervous. He threw so hard during his first days in camp that he immediately developed a sore arm. Then, when he was able to pitch batting practice, he was so wild that he chased the hitters out of the cage. Finally Joe Becker, the Dodgers' pitching coach, led Sandy behind some barracks where the players slept and let him work out there, alone.

From the very first, Becker seemed to understand Koufax. As pitching coach he had more time than anybody else to work with him. This gave him the opportunity to study Koufax's special problems and to try and work out solutions to them. Sandy and Becker were to form a solid relationship over the next several years.

Meanwhile the Dodgers, bound by a rule that forbade teams to farm out high-priced bonus players, were faced with keeping Koufax on the roster. The Dodgers of 1955 were pennant contenders and Sandy took up valuable space on the 25-man roster. Naturally, he didn't get to pitch much that season. He appeared in just 12 games, winning two and losing two. The Dodgers swept the National League to take the pennant and then went on to win their very first World Series. In the Series, Sandy was as much a spectator as any of the 30,000-odd fans who squeezed into Ebbets Field.

The next several years were frustrating to Koufax.

Under the watchful eye of pitching coach Joe Becker, Sandy works out at the Dodgers' spring training camp.

For every step of progress, he seemed to take three giant steps backward. What hurt even more was that he had brief flashes of brilliance. These would raise his hopes, which would then be dashed to pieces in the next game.

In the second start of his rookie year, he had shut out the Reds on two hits and had struck out 14 men. But he was putting everything he had on the ball instead of throwing easily. Overthrowing caused him to be wild, and the wildness made him desperate.

Koufax spent the winter of 1957 in the army. By the time he rejoined the Dodgers the following spring they had become the Los Angeles Dodgers. But as far as he was concerned that was about the only thing that had changed. He continued to ride the bench as much as before. One day he took his complaints to Buzzy Bavasi, the Dodgers' general manager. "I want to pitch and I'm not getting the chance," he said.

"How can you pitch when you can't get the side out?" Bavasi said.

Koufax did manage to get into 40 ball games that season and broke even with an 11–11 record. But the following year, 1959, proved to be an important milestone in his career. In June he started a game against the Phillies and struck out 16 batters. Two months later, on August 31, he fanned 18 Giants to break Dizzy Dean's National League record of 17 strikeouts, established in 1933. He also tied the major league record set by Bob Feller in 1943.

Although he wound up the 1959 season with an unimpressive 8–6 record, Koufax was given his first World Series start that fall. But he lost a 1–0 heartbreaker to Bob Shaw and the Chicago White Sox. Sandy was still far from being satisfied by his "progress."

In 1960 Sandy fell off to an 8–13 record. After six big league seasons, his pitching record stood at 38 wins and 40 defeats. However, 1960 was the last year in which Sandy Koufax would be just another promising pitcher.

The following spring, he was riding one day in the Dodger bus in Florida. Seated beside him was his roommate, Norm Sherry, a catcher. Sherry knew what was behind the brooding silence of his roommate, and he finally decided to make an effort to break through the wall.

"You know what I think?" Sherry said.

"No, what do you think?" Sandy answered.

"I think your troubles would be solved if you would just throw easier," Sherry said. "Throw more change-ups, and just try to get the ball over."

Koufax sighed. He had been over that route hundreds of times before. Everyone from Alston and Becker right down to the batboy had been trying to convince him that, if he just threw naturally instead of trying to throw each pitch past the batter, he would be better able to control his pitches. But on this particular spring day the advice really seemed to get through to him for the first time. He decided to try to follow it. Opposing teams have been regretting his decision ever since.

Koufax worked at getting his pitching into a rhythm, and he permitted himself to experiment with it in games. He got off to a fast start at the outset of the season by winning six of his first seven games. He was finding the plate more often than not and he was striking out the hitters. As Sandy has since observed, "I used to try to throw each pitch harder than the previous one. There was no need for it. I found out that if I take it easy and throw naturally, the ball goes just as fast. I found that my control improved and the strikeouts would take care of themselves."

In 1961 Sandy led the league in strikeouts with 269, while winning 18 games and losing 13. He was becoming a pitcher instead of just a thrower. But he still was not satisfied. He continued to work on his rhythm, checking himself the minute he felt he was beginning to overthrow again. Some baseball superstars are born and others are self-made. Koufax falls into the latter category.

Sandy's first real brush with fame occurred on the night of June 30, 1962. Two months earlier he had struck out 18 Chicago Cubs, becoming the first major league pitcher to achieve that feat twice. But this night in June was even more special. The Dodgers were playing the New York Mets in Dodger Stadium. Koufax mowed down the Mets without giving them a hit. He struck out 13 hitters and gave up just five walks. It was Sandy's first no-hitter.

Incredibly, he followed this with a no-hitter in each of his next three seasons. His 1965 no-hitter was his masterpiece, though. He pitched a "perfect game" against the Cubs. Not one man reached base—27 up and 27 down. In addition, he struck out 14 batters. It was the ninth perfect game in baseball history, and Koufax became the first man ever to hurl four no-hitters.

Koufax became a 20-game winner for the first time in 1963. He won 25 games and lost five. He led the league in strikeouts (for the second time) with 306, and he turned in the lowest earned-run average

—a stingy 1.88.

Koufax's performance was all the more remarkable, because he had come back from an injury which at one point threatened to end his career. The injury dated back to the 1962 season. Sometime in July of that year he began to experience a numbness in the tip of his left forefinger. Gradually, his finger began to blister and pieces of flesh would peel off, making it extremely painful for him even to touch anything, much less try to hold a baseball. Specialists tried treating his finger with drugs. Although they were able to reduce the soreness, they were unable to explain the origin of the trouble. The season was curtailed for Koufax, and he pitched only 184 innings for a 14–7 record. Needless to say, the Dodgers' hopes for a pennant vanished.

Sandy's recovery in 1963 was complete, as his 25–5 record indicated. He won both his starts against the Yankees in the World Series as the Dodgers took four in a row. At the end of the season Koufax won the Cy Young Award as baseball's best pitcher, in addition to the Most Valuable Player Award in the National League. The following year his record was 19–5, and he led the league for the third consecutive time with a 1.74 earned-run average.

In 1963 a recovered Koufax pitched brilliantly against the Yanks in the World Series.

Then in 1965 Sandy received another severe jolt. The doctors discovered that he had traumatic arthritis in his left elbow. There is no known cure for this type of arthritis. Sandy took the blow philosophically. Even though he realized that his arm could give out at any time, he refused to pamper himself or feel sorry for himself.

In the meantime, he continued to pitch with the same brilliance he had shown in past seasons. The only departure from his normal routine was the icewater baths he began to take after every game in order to help reduce the swelling. He also received periodic injections of a drug to keep the arm as sound as possible. In spite of his arthritis, Sandy had perhaps his finest year in 1965, winning 26 games, to lead both leagues in victories. He also worked 336 innings—the highest total of his career—and was the earned-run leader for the fourth consecutive year with a 2.04 average.

In the final week of the 1966 season, the Dodgers were battling to hold their slim lead, which was being whittled down by both the Giants and Pirates. Koufax pitched a masterful 2–1 win over the Cardinals to maintain a two-and-a-half-game lead. It was his twenty-sixth win of the season and it should have been his last before the World Series. But the

Dodgers lost to the Phillies the next day, Friday, and on Saturday they were rained out. So they had to play a double-header on the final Sunday of the year.

The Giants had taken two games from the Pirates on Saturday so they trailed the Dodgers by only two games. Los Angeles needed to win one of their two remaining Sunday games with the Phils to insure their possession of the pennant. If they failed, they would be forced into a play-off with the Giants.

The Phillies won the opener, 4–3, so Walt Alston had to come back with Koufax after just two days of rest. Sandy answered the call and pitched the clinching game.

After Sandy had won the 1966 pennant by beating the Giants while pitching with a slipped vertebra, he had to face one last ordeal—the World Series. The Dodgers had already lost the Series opener to the Baltimore Orioles. Now it was up to Koufax to even the score. Everybody was certain that he would turn the score in favor of the Dodgers. He had done it so many times in the past. Surely that magnificent left arm would do it once more. After all, this was only his third start in eight days and his forty-first of the season.

Though Sandy was obviously tired, and was forcing his pitches, he managed to match scoreless innings with young Jim Palmer until the fifth. Then Sandy was undone, but not through his own playing. Outfielder Willie Davis seemed to be settling under a fly ball and then—some thought it was because of the sun—unexpectedly lost it and the ball dropped to the ground. Then Davis lost another fly ball. Before the inning was over, he had committed three errors and the Orioles had scored three runs on their way to a 6–0 victory.

The Series was still three days away from the inevitable, but with that game all the air had seemed to leave the Dodgers' sails. The Orioles cruised to a four-game sweep of the Series.

The years are filled with images of Sandy Koufax, in victory and in defeat. But perhaps the image that will last longest in peoples' minds will be the simple and human gesture he made after Davis' horrible inning. Sandy rushed past his solicitous teammates to where Davis was trying to hide in the shadows of the dugout and he threw both his arms around him and said, "It's okay, Willie. Don't let it get you down."

This is the stamp of the man that is Koufax, on the field or off. The same quality marked a momentous press conference called by Sandy himself some six weeks after the 1966 World Series.

"I'm retiring from baseball," he announced, confirming what many had suspected: that he might permanently injure his arthritic left arm if he continued to pitch. The Dodgers had hoped he would delay his announcement, perhaps even try another season. But Sandy, whose salary of $125,000 made him the highest-paid pitcher in history, would not prolong the agony, or the suspense.

"I felt," he said, "that I was being too devious when my friends kept asking me what I was going to do. I didn't want to lie and I didn't want to keep on being devious."

Pills, shots and therapy could not sustain the greatest left-hander of this era, perhaps of any era. So at the age of 31, in the prime of his career, the once-wild pitcher from Brooklyn reluctantly said farewell to baseball.

Harmon Killebrew 4

The incoming pitch was aimed directly at Harmon Killebrew's head. As he dropped to the ground, the ball hummed by his ear, missing his head by an inch.

Killebrew got up slowly, smacking the dust off his pants, his broad face calm. From the stands came the boos of Minnesota fans expressing their anger at the pitcher. But Killebrew said nothing. As one of the most consistent home-run hitters in baseball, he knows he must pay a price for his home runs. The price is having to duck balls thrown at his head by pitchers anxious to keep him off balance at the plate.

He stepped into the batter's box again. In came the next pitch. Kellebrew swung, and at the solid sound of wood against ball the Minnesota crowd stood up, roaring their approval. They knew the sound of a home run. The ball soared high into the blue sky, and then plunged down into the left-field stands.

Since Killebrew became a big league regular in 1959, only Willie Mays has hit more homers than he has. From 1959 through 1966, Mays hit 326 home runs and Killebrew hit 325. But not even Mays (who has come up to bat more often) could hit them at a faster rate. In fact, only one man in baseball history—the great Babe Ruth—has smacked home runs more frequently than Killebrew. During his career Ruth averaged one home run for every 11.8 times he batted. In contrast, Willie Mays has hit one homer for every 15 at-bats and Mickey Mantle has hit one for every 13 at-bats. During the first eight years of his career, Harmon Killebrew hit a home run every 12.2 times he batted —a close second to Ruth.

Killebrew played his first big league season for the old Washington Senators, the team that moved west in 1961 to become the Minnesota Twins. The Senators played in Griffith Stadium, where the left-field fence was 388 feet from home. Killebrew once hit a ball that came within two rows of leaving the Stadium. Only Mickey Mantle has ever hit a ball out of that park, and he hit with the aid of a 40-mile-per-hour tailwind.

Great hitters like Mays and Mantle are powerfully built men who have the muscles of weight-lifters. But even these powerful men talk with awe of Killebrew's strength.

"He's so strong he muscles a pitch out of the ball park," says Mantle. "He's strong, strong, strong," Bob Allison, a teammate, once said. Allison stands 6 feet 4 inches and weighs 220 pounds while Killebrew stands only 5 feet 11 inches and weighs 215 pounds. But when Allison looked at the tree-trunk arms of Killebrew he shook his head in admiration.

A Yankee pitcher, Steve Hamilton, once told how he pitches to Killebrew. "He is a pull hitter," said Hamilton, "so I pitch him low and away. You throw him strikes on the outside corner and he can't pull the ball because it's too far out and he can't lift the ball because it's too low.

"But I remember one game, I got this pitch low and outside, just where I wanted it, and he swung. At worse I figured it was a base hit into right field, But he reached for that down-and-out pitch and hit it over the right-field fence. That's what I call overpowering the ball."

Killebrew has led the American League in home runs three years in a row—1962, 1963 and 1964. Early in spring training in 1965, a writer looked up the record and told Harmon: "If you win the home-run title again, you'll be edging close to Babe Ruth's record of six in a row."

Killebrew only nodded. He is quiet and soft-spoken, and he dislikes talking about his home-run feats. His wife once said, "I can always tell when he has hit another home run. He comes into the house looking sheepish."

In spite of Killebrew's home runs, the Minnesota Twins from 1961 to 1964 were a second-division team in the American League. In 1964 they finished a dismal sixth. One day during 1965 spring training the Twins' manager, Sam Mele, was talking to Harmon at the batting cage.

"Harmon," said Mele, "you hit .270 last year. Do you think you could get your average up close to .300?"

"I don't think so," said Killebrew. "I'm not fast enough to run out any infield hits. Of course, I could cut down on my swing. I'd hit fewer home runs, but I'd probably strike out a lot less. Then, maybe, I'd get more base hits. The question is: Would that be helping the ball club?"

Mele thought that it would help, so Killebrew agreed to try to cut down on his swing.

Actually, his promise to alter his swing was one that might affect his whole career. He was being paid $50,000 a year to hit home runs. If he hit singles instead of home runs and the Twins won the pennant, he would go on earning $50,000. But if the Twins lost and Killebrew was just another singles hitter, he might not be worth $50,000 any longer.

Still, he stuck to his promise in spring training and cut down on his swing, lining out singles and doubles and striking out less. Near the end of March, Mele moved him from left field to first base. Originally, he had been a third baseman. The anxiety caused by fielding two very different positions had impaired his ability to concentrate at bat.

"You'll play first base this season all the way," Mele told Killebrew. "This is a promise. No more moving around for you. You learn to play first base and then you can concentrate on that new swing."

At the beginning of the season the Twins moved into first place. By May the team was still on top and the pressure on Mele was mounting. Each day he had to post his strongest starting line-up. On the

Harmon Killebrew waits expectantly for the ball as a Dodger player slides into third.

bench he had first baseman Don Mincher, a poor hitter against left-handed pitching, but a home-run slugger against right-handed pitching.

One night the Twins were scheduled to face a right-hander. In the dugout Killebrew walked over to Mele.

"I know you'd like to get Don's bat into the game," he told his manager. "I'll play another position so Don can play first base, if it will help."

Mele stared at his stocky slugger. "But how about the promise I made—that I wouldn't switch you?"

"Forget it," said Killebrew.

He went back to left field and Mincher went to first base. Later Killebrew played third when the Twins faced right-handers and first when they faced left-handers. The day-to-day shifting hurt him at the plate; by mid-season he had hit only 15 home runs. But he was now overwhelming opposing teams with clutch base hits. His average climbed to .290, but even that didn't tell the full story. His batting average with runners in scoring position was .379. The year before, when he had been swinging for homers, his average with men on second or third was only .235.

With Killebrew driving in runs, the Twins hung on to first through July and August. And as the team drew near the close of the season, a player named Rich Rollins found out something about the Twins' star that no statistic will ever reveal. Rollins had been the team's regular third baseman, but when Killebrew volunteered to shift from first, Rollins was benched.

"Look, Rich," Harmon said to Rollins one day, "I didn't realize I would cost you a regular job. I'm sorry that happened. But I'm sure you'll be playing regular soon. You're too good to be kept on the bench very long."

"Never mind," said Rollins. "We're winning, aren't we? That's the big thing."

Later Rollins told someone what Killebrew had said. "It was a real big boost for me," said Rollins. "My morale was kind of low. And it was something Harmon didn't have to do."

A spirited Rollins did come back to play third when Killebrew was badly injured in a collision at first base. The injury kept "the Killer" out of the line-up for a month. Without him, said sports writers, the Twins would fold. But the Twins, fired up by the sacrifices Killebrew had made for the team, kept on winning. When he came back the Twins were still clinging to first place, and they held on to win the pennant.

The Twins' slugging star winces in pain as he lies on the ground after a collision with a Baltimore base runner.

Killebrew, stiff from his injury, hit poorly in the last few weeks of the season. His average faded to .269 and he finished with only 25 home runs. But Sam Mele knew that the statistics did not tell the whole story. He knew how Killebrew had sacrificed himself and his home-run title for the team. Near the end of the season Mele said to him: "Harmon, you're still the best home run hitter in the game, but you're something else, too. You're a team ballplayer, and in my book that's the biggest title there is."

In the World Series the Twins met the Los Angeles Dodgers. The two teams battled to the final game, tied at three games apiece. In the last game, the great Sandy Koufax mowed down the Twins through eight innings. The Twins came up in the bottom of the ninth, trailing 2–0.

Koufax retired the first Twin and then Killebrew came to bat. The Minnesota crowd stood and pleaded for him to come through to save the Series. Koufax delivered a stinging fast ball. Killebrew swung and the crowd roared as he connected for a line-drive base hit. Now the tying run stood at the plate.

But Koufax struck out the next two Twins and Killebrew was left on base as the Dodgers ran triumphantly off the field. The Minnesota crowd filed silently out of the stadium. Their team had lost the Series, but they knew that it was not Killebrew's fault. He had given the Twins their chance.

Harmon Killebrew was born on June 29, 1936, in Payette, Idaho. He attended Payette High School, where he was a B-plus student and won a dozen letters in football, basketball and baseball.

In football he steered the team as a T-formation quarterback and the University of Oregon offered him a football scholarship. Although Harmon was more interested in baseball, only a few big league scouts came to look at him, and none seemed very much interested. Harmon decided to accept the football scholarship. However, through the help of Herman Welker, United States Senator from Idaho, Harmon's future turned out differently.

In Washington, D. C., Welker had heard about Harmon's long home runs for Payette High. A few years earlier Senator Welker had tipped off the Pittsburgh Pirates about a young Idaho pitcher named Vernon Law, and the Pirates signed the boy.

"Gee, Senator," complained Clark Griffith, owner of the Senators, "Law has become a great pitcher for the Pirates. Why don't you tip *us* off about players like that?"

Senator Welker agreed that the next time he spotted a potential star he would tell Griffith about him.

One summer day in 1953 Clark Griffith's phone rang. "Hello, Clark," said the voice at the other end. "This is Senator Welker. There's a boy out in Payette . . ."

A few days later Ossie Bluege, a Senator scout, came to Payette. He saw Harmon play three games. In 12 times at bat, the right-handed Killebrew knocked out 11 hits, including three triples and four home runs.

Bluege hastened to phone Griffith. "This boy is sensational," he said. "But he has a football scholarship. We'll have to bid high for him."

The very next day Harmon signed a Washington Senator contract for $30,000—a huge bonus at that time.

Harmon, only 17 years old, came to Washington for the 1954 season. There he was greeted as the home-run hitter from the mountains. However, the rules of that time required that he stay with the Senators for two years because he had been signed for a bonus. This meant that he would languish on the bench instead of playing and getting experience in the minors.

The Senators' manager, Bucky Harris (right), talks to his new 17-year-old bonus player.

The Senators' enthusiasm soon faded away, for this big kid from Idaho didn't look much like a star. He fielded balls awkwardly and threw so stiffly that manager Bucky Harris said, "He throws like a girl."

He looked like anything but a ballplayer according to Johnny Pesky, then a Senator player. "But he listened and learned. He remembered what you told him."

From 1956 to 1958 Harmon bounced between the Senators and the minors, never quite sure where he would be playing next. Once, in the summer of 1957, he thought he had made the big club. Then one afternoon, as the team boarded a bus in Cleveland, a Senator official tapped him on the shoulder. "You'll have to get off the bus, Harmon," he said. "They're sending you to Chattanooga."

A steady rain began to drum down on the sidewalk outside the bus. As the Senators watched, Harmon searched the bus for his bag. "Look," said third baseman Eddie Yost, "you'll get soaked. Wait'll we get you a cab."

"No, thanks," said Killebrew. "I'll walk."

He picked up his heavy bag, stepped out of the bus into the driving rain, and began to trudge toward the train depot. The Senators watched him through the rain-splattered windows, but Harmon did not look back.

In 1959 he came back to the big leagues to stay and caused a sensation with his booming home runs. Harmon hit 42 homers in 1959, 31 in 1960, 46 in 1961, 48 in 1962, and 45 in 1963.

After the 1963 season Killebrew underwent an operation on his knee. The operation was successful and he returned the following spring eager to begin the season. Instead of leading the league in homers, however, he fell into an unusual slump. In early May, with a .167 average, he was benched by manager Sam Mele. Four days later Mele put the rested Killebrew back in the line-up. In 16 games he hit 10 home runs and added almost 100 points to his average.

Killebrew hit 49 home runs in 1964. But in 1965, when he cut down his swing to help win a pennant, he hit only 25. In 1966, when Mele asked him to go for the long ball again, he raised his total to 39. His batting average over the years has varied between a low of .242 and a high of .288. In only three of the years from 1959 through 1966 did Killebrew fail to drive in at least 100 runs.

Killebrew has not changed much during his baseball career. He is still the quiet, unassuming mountain boy who goes about setting major league rec-

Killebrew's Minnesota teammates congratulate him after he slams out another homer.

ords without fanfare. Most sports writers have abandoned the practice of giving him colorful names like "Killer" because such names do not seem to fit his personality.

However, Killebrew's calm exterior has not prevented the Twins from appreciating his excellence. Catcher Earl Battey once summed up his value to the club. "This team without Killebrew," said Battey, "is like a man dressed up for a formal affair with white tie and tails and wearing muddy shoes. Harmon puts us all in bigger shoes and adds the sparkle."

Juan Marichal   5

Right from the start the San Francisco Giants knew Juan Marichal was something special. In 1958, when they sent him to Michigan City, Indiana, in the Midwest League, he led the league's pitchers with 21 victories and a splendid 1.87 earned-run average. Juan was 20 years old, playing his first season in professional baseball.

The next year the Giants moved him up to Springfield, Massachusetts, in the Eastern League. With 18 wins and a 2.39 earned-run average, he was again the league's best pitcher.

Then in 1960 the Giants sent him to Tacoma,

Washington, in the Pacific Coast League. This league is as high as a player can go before reaching the majors. But even so the Giants didn't let Marichal finish the season there. His record was 11–5 by early July, so they decided that young Juan had had all the minor league seasoning he would ever need. They summoned him to San Francisco, hoping that he could help them to win a pennant.

For 10 days Marichal pitched batting practice for the Giants. Finally, Manager Bill Rigney found a spot where he felt he could use the new pitcher. "Do you feel ready to make a start for this club?" Rigney asked Juan.

Juan smiled. "Ready?" he said. "Sure! Why not?"

That was the kind of answer Rigney liked to hear. So, on a cold, windy night in San Francisco, Juan Marichal's name appeared on a major league line-up card for the first time. Before the night was over, the Giants realized it would not be the last time.

The Giants' opponents, the Philadelphia Phillies, watched Juan warm up on the side lines and they did not like what they saw. Marichal, a 6-foot, 185-pound right-hander, reared back so far that the knuckles of his pitching hand almost scraped the mound. He kicked his left leg out and up—higher than his head. When he fired the ball from behind

Giant Juan Marichal about to fire the ball from behind "the big kick."

the big kick, the batter had difficulty seeing it. And Juan would finish each pitch by falling so far forward that he seemed to be halfway to home plate.

The first time the Phillies came to bat they found out what was in store for them. Bobby Del Greco and Tony Taylor, the first two men to face Marichal, both struck out. Then Juan got the next batter, too. That opening inning was a strong hint of what was to come. Inning after inning, Marichal mixed up his fast ball, curve and slider like a veteran as he mowed down the Phillies.

Marichal showed the Philadelphia hitters one other pitch, too, and it baffled them more than any other. It was a fast ball thrown at about five-sixths of its expected speed. Juan had no name for this pitch. He delivered it exactly like his fast ball, but reduced its speed just a bit. The hitter, thinking that a full-fledged fast ball was on the way, would swing too soon and miss the pitch by a foot, which was very embarrassing.

Going into the eighth inning, Juan did not have to be told that he had a no-hitter going. No one would have mentioned it anyway, because baseball superstition forbids it. He got the first two batters out and then Phillie catcher Clay Dalrymple was sent up to pinch-hit. Dalrymple lashed out at a low, slow curve and hit it sharply past Juan into short center field. It was a clean hit—the only one the Phillies got all night. In his major league debut, Juan Marichal had pitched a 2–0, one-hit shutout.

Reporters flocked into the Giant clubhouse to find out more about the cool, overpowering rookie. They found out, first of all, that Juan could not speak English very well. First baseman Orlando Cepeda had to interpret for him. The reporters also discovered that Marichal had the confidence of a ten-year veteran. "He says he doesn't even know the name of the guy who got the hit," Cepeda reported. "He also says he expected to win. He always expects to win."

Being a winner was second nature to Juan. This trait could be traced back to his boyhood days in the Dominican Republic, a small country in the Caribbean. He was born in Laguna Verde on October 20, 1937. While growing up there, Juan had to prove himself many times. One day, for example, he went diving for lobster. He could not afford aqualung equipment and diving without it was dangerous, even for an expert skin-diver like Juan. But Juan went anyway, gashing his legs on the coral growths where lobsters hide. At the end of the day Juan had caught 40 lobsters. They weighed up to nine pounds apiece, and, since lobster is not cheap, Juan earned a considerable amount of money.

Baseball is the national sport in the Dominican Republic and Juan began to play at a very early age. He started out as a shortstop, but when he was just 13 his older brother, Gonzolo, a former semi-pro player, taught him to throw a curve ball. Juan began to study books with stories and pictures of famous pitchers and decided that he too would become a pitcher.

After high school, he served in the Dominican air force for two years and developed his pitching skills against some good competition. While in the air force, Marichal impressed a scout for the Giants, who in turn told famed scout Alex Pompez about Juan. Pompez wrote the Giants and advised them to send Juan a contract.

"Have you seen Marichal yourself?" the Giants wrote back.

Pompez said he had not, but since it would take only $500 to sign him, why argue.

Looking back on the matter today, Jack Schwarz, head of the Giants' farm system, is still amazed. "Even at $500 I was worried," says Schwarz. "All we had was a vague report that the kid had been a shortstop, had turned pitcher and had a lot of stuff. It makes me shudder to think how skeptical we were and how we might have passed him up. Pompez didn't push it hard. Heck, he'd never laid eyes on Marichal and was too busy to bother. I call Juan our mail-order ballplayer."

Leaving the Dominican Republic for the first time was a little frightening for the shy Marichal, especially when Pompez warned him that some people in the United States might treat him badly because of the color of his skin. Juan found this hard to believe, but he learned quickly. Driving through some Southern states while on his way from spring training camp to Indiana, Juan was told for the first time in his life that he could not eat in any restaurant he chose.

Though the color problem in the United States was bewildering to Marichal, baseball certainly wasn't. As previously mentioned, he quickly outgrew his first two minor league teams. During his year at Springfield, Manager Andy Gilbert submitted the following report to the Giants: "I've looked and looked and I can't find *anything* he can't do. In a year he'll be winning for the Big Club, I honestly believe."

Gilbert was wrong. Marichal was winning for the

Big Club in half a season. He followed up his one-hit debut in 1960 with two more victories and finished the season with a 6–2 record. The next year he had a good but not a great 13–10 record and a 3.89 earned-run average. On the whole, Marichal was making fairly smooth progress, both on and off the field. He had moved into a boarding house with some other Latin American players and was having a fine time. The house was owned by Blanche Johnson, who taught the players how to speak English and instructed them about American customs. Each morning she made the ballplayers practice their English and when they would occasionally slip into Spanish, she would grab a dish towel and chase them around the house. They loved it, for they realized that Blanche Johnson really cared about them.

Marichal also had someone else who cared. Her name was Alma Rosa and she was back home in the Dominican Republic. During 1962 spring training in Phoenix, Arizona, Juan missed her more and more. He wanted to marry her. "So marry her in October when the season's over," Manager Al Dark advised his sad, young pitcher.

"No," said Juan. "I want her to leave the Dominican Republic right away. There is much danger down there."

Juan was not exaggerating about the danger. The country's dictator had been assassinated the year before and different political groups were fighting for control.

"Why not have her come to Phoenix and marry here?" Dark asked Marichal.

"Because," said Juan, "she cannot get a permit to leave the country unless she has a husband over here."

Dark knew that a happy ballplayer is usually a winning ballplayer so he gave Marichal permission to fly home. He also advised the young player to do some running every day while he was down there. Plenty of road work would keep him in shape.

"Don't worry," said Juan, grinning. "I run all the way from the airport to Alma Rosa's house and then to the preacher and back to the airport with her!"

Marichal returned five days later, a happily married man. To thank his manager for making it all possible, he vowed to pitch a great opening-day game. And he kept his promise by beating Milwaukee on three hits, 6–0.

Things continued to go well for most of the 1962 season and by early September Juan had won 17 games. Then he injured his foot badly on a fielding play and was hospitalized. When he was released, his foot still bothered him, and he felt he could not pitch. The Giants, however, were fighting desperately for the National League pennant and could not afford to have a man like Marichal sitting on the side lines. On the next-to-last game of the season, Juan, much against his wishes, was told to pitch. He was beaten by Houston and it was rumored later that he felt the Giants had risked a permanent injury to him for the sake of one game.

The Giants won the pennant anyway and faced the Yankees in the World Series. Pitching in the fourth game, Juan had a 2–0 lead after four innings. Then bad luck struck again. While he was trying to bunt against Whitey Ford, his right index finger got in the way of the ball. His finger was smashed and he had to leave the game.

Juan hoped to pitch again if the Series went to seven games, but Dark seemed to be annoyed with him. He told reporters that Marichal wouldn't pitch again in the Series "even if it rained for a week."

Marichal was crushed. "What did I do wrong?" he asked friends. "I looked bad against Houston, sure, but my foot is not well. Against the Yankees, didn't I strike out four men in four innings and give no runs?"

He was still in Dark's doghouse the following spring. He showed up late for training and carried more than the normal 185 pounds on his 6-foot frame. But once the 1963 season really began, all was forgiven. Marichal started off well and it was obvious that he had developed into the best right-handed pitcher in baseball. For those who still doubted it, Marichal put together two games within a month's time that were both unforgettable.

The first came on June 15 in San Francisco, where the Giants were playing Houston. Before the game Juan gave teammate Willie "Stretch" McCovey quite a surprise. "I think I do something different today," said Juan. "I change my windup and use the number two motion. What you say, Stretch?"

"I think you're nuts," said McCovey. Willie had a point. Marichal has just won five games in a row, so why make changes.

But Juan remembered that Houston had hit him pretty hard in the last few games the two teams had played. He suspected that Houston's hitters had been reading his grip and predicting which pitch was coming. So instead of the usual delivery, Marichal decided to bring his hands to his belt and pivot from there. He told McCovey to play deeper in left field than usual, in case the new delivery did not work against the right-handed hitters.

His strategy worked perfectly. He upset the timing of Houston's batters, retiring the other side without a hit, inning after inning. In the seventh inning, however, what Marichal had feared nearly happened. Right-handed Carl Warwick drove the ball deep to left field. But McCovey was playing farther back as Marichal had suggested so he was in position to make the catch. As it turned out, Warwick's fly was the closest thing to a hit that Houston got all day. Juan pitched his first no-hitter. It was also the first Giant no-hitter in 34 years.

Perhaps the most important result of his no-hitter was Manager Dark's wholehearted praise. "When you really have to win a game," said Dark, "Marichal gives you confidence. He thrives on competition. The tougher the situation, the better he is. For a 25-year-old, he amazes me with his command of a variety of deliveries."

A couple of weeks later, Marichal put on an even more amazing performance. Though he didn't pitch a no-hitter, he beat the great Warren Spahn in one of the most spectacular pitching duels of all time. Inning after inning rolled by and neither the Giants nor the Braves could score a run. Amazingly, the longer Marichal pitched, the stronger he seemed.

As he walks off the field after pitching his first no-hitter, Marichal raises his hat to acknowledge the fans' applause.

From the eighth through the thirteenth inning he retired 16 hitters in a row.

The titanic struggle was mentally harder on Dark than it appeared to be on Marichal. Dark kept telling himself he ought to take Marichal out rather than risk an injury to him, but every time the manager looked at Marichal he could see that his pitcher was showing no pressure and even seemed to be enjoying himself. After the game Dark said he had had the conviction that Marichal was bound to beat Spahn.

Dark was right. In the bottom of the 16th inning, with the score still 0–0, Willie Mays came to bat. He hit a home run and the game was over; the score: Giants 1, Braves 0. For Juan Marichal it was perhaps the most remarkable victory of his career.

The 1963 season was Marichal's breakthrough as a 20-game winner. He won 25 games, lost only eight, struck out 248 hitters and had an earned-run average of 2.41. The 1963 season was not just a matter of luck, because he had similar years in 1964, 1965, and 1966. In none of those four years did he win fewer than 21 games, strike out fewer than 206 men, walk more than 61 men or have an earned-run average higher than 2.48.

These achievements should have brought Marichal great happiness, and they did to a degree. But there was also an emptiness caused by the unrest in his homeland. For several years the Dominican Republic was torn by civil war and violent political hatreds. Even Marichal became a target for insults by his countrymen. When injuries prevented his playing in the winter league in the Republic, people turned against him.

One night he was attacked by several men in a club in Santo Domingo. They said he had become a swellhead who was full of American ideas. Even his wife was threatened during the winter that followed the 1963 season, and one day Juan needed police protection at the ballpark.

Fortunately this was only a temporary condition. As soon as stability was restored to the Dominican Republic, Marichal's countrymen once again idolized him. They had to be proud of the man who had overcome racial prejudice and the difficulties of life in a strange country to become baseball's greatest right-handed pitcher.

Hank Aaron 6

During a game with the Pittsburgh Pirates late in the 1966 season, the Atlanta Braves were leading, 3–2. In the bottom of the eighth, sleepy-eyed Henry Aaron walked up to hit for the Braves. As he took up his relaxed stance, a voice from the Pittsburgh dugout boomed, "Hey, Aaron!" Hank didn't even turn his head, and he continued to ignore the additional taunts that his opponents directed at his back.

The count ran to 3 and 2 when Aaron took a pitch he liked and hit a long drive well back into the left-field stands for his forty-second home run of the season.

Coming around third, Hank gestured toward the Pittsburgh dugout, asking them how they liked the homer. Needless to say, the Pirates were not very appreciative, but Atlanta fans cheered the feat. Aaron's run had helped defeat Pittsburgh that day.

Later, Aaron admitted that those yells from the Pirates' dugout got under his skin and woke him up. They agitated him, and "I don't like to be agitated," he said.

A similar incident occurred in a game with the Giants early in Aaron's career. In his first trip to the plate Hank had doubled off Johnny Antonelli. As Aaron dug in for his second at-bat, Antonelli shouted at him from the mound, "You can afford to lose some teeth, you so-and-so."

"But can *you?*" retorted Aaron.

Antonelli wound up carefully and uncorked a high, inside fast ball. Hank smashed it for a 450-foot home run. When the day was over he had hit three homers and had driven in seven runs. The Braves won, 13–3.

It has always been like that for Hank Aaron, ever since he joined the Braves in Milwaukee in 1954. When challenged or insulted, he almost invariably has replied with a long-distance wallop.

Whether in Milwaukee or Atlanta—where the

team moved in 1966—Hank has thrilled the crowds with his batting exploits. One of his rivals, Tommy Davis of the Los Angeles Dodgers, has called him "the best man in the world with a bat," and many baseball experts agree. It is difficult to argue with Hank's lifetime batting average, which is near .320.

Aaron has always been more than just a pure hitter or a talented, all-round ballplayer. He is an intense competitor, and that is what has lifted him to elite status as one of baseball's superstars.

Hank's most memorable feat came on September 23, 1957, in a game with the St. Louis Cardinals. The Braves needed only one more victory to give Milwaukee its first pennant since the franchise had shifted from Boston in 1953. The score was 2-2 in the eleventh inning when Aaron came up to hit against Billy Muffet. Hank knew that Muffet had not given up a homer all year, and he savored the challenge as he stepped into the batter's box. Muffet's first pitch was a curve and Aaron's bat was a blur as it whipped around. At the 402-foot sign in center field, the Cards' Wally Moon leaped for the hit and came down empty-handed. It was a home run and Milwaukee had won the pennant.

In the World Series that followed, Hank was setting himself up for a pitch when catcher Yogi Berra

Milwaukee's jubilant Braves lift Hank Aaron onto their shoulders in honor of the slugger's pennant-clinching homer.

looked up at him and said, "Hey, you're holding the bat wrong. You should hold it so that you can read the label."

"Didn't come here to read," replied Aaron as he lined a base hit to left field.

Hank hit .393 for the Series and the Braves beat the Yankees, four games to three. He also won the Most Valuable Player Award that year.

Baseball has been a succession of glorious moments for the guy who came out of Mobile, Alabama, in 1952, with an explosive bat. Aaron has averaged as high as .355 in a big-league season and has won two National League batting championships. He has led his league in home runs three times and has topped the National League in runs-batted-in-four times. Even in 1966, when his .279 average was the lowest since his rookie year, Aaron held up his end. He hit 44 homers and drove in 127 runs.

The road to all this success began quite modestly for Aaron. In Mobile, Alabama, when kids chose up to play on the bumpy sandlots, they always wanted Hank on their side. Despite his athletic success, however, he did not mix with the other boys.

"I wasn't much of a kid to hang out with the gang," says Hank. "I hung around home a lot and read books at the library."

He went to Central High School, then switched to a private school. Both had one drawback—no baseball team. So he played softball and went out for football. He played halfback and end, and one year he led the Central team in touchdowns. But he quit the game. "I wanted to get into pro sports and knew baseball was my only chance," Aaron says. "I had to concentrate on one game or I'd never have made it."

Even then, he hit the ball with a seemingly effortless swing and he was becoming a good infielder. Hank was just 15 when he was signed off the sandlots to play semi-pro ball. He collected three dollars a game.

One day he heard that the Dodgers were holding a tryout in Mobile, so he hurried over with high expectations. The scouts lined the boys up for fielding drill and, when Hank moved in to take his turn, a bigger boy shoved him aside. Aaron lost his chance and went home crestfallen.

If the Dodger scouts didn't get the opportunity to size up Aaron's talent, there were other baseball men who did. Bunny Downs, road secretary of the

Indianapolis Clowns in the Negro American League, watched Hank playing semi-pro ball one night and could hardly wait until the game was completed. He rushed up to Aaron and said, "How would you like $200 a month to play for the Clowns?"

"I'd like it fine," said Hank, "but I doubt that my ma will. She's set on me going to college."

Downs knew that Henry respected his mother's wishes, so he spent a good deal of time talking to Estella Aaron. She finally agreed to let her boy sign after he had graduated from high school. "I couldn't believe it would happen to me so fast," Aaron said.

So in the spring of 1952, 18-year-old Henry Aaron stood in the Mobile railroad station, saying good-by to his family. Henry was scared and they were all crying as he walked toward the train with his one flimsy suitcase and some sandwiches his mother had made for him. He never dreamed that in two short years he would be a first-string outfielder in the major leagues.

Physically, he didn't look like much when he reported to the Clowns' camp in Winston-Salem, North Carolina. And his new uniform seemed a size too big on his slender body. In addition, the team had not given him a windbreaker when equipment was issued, so the chilly spring air made him shiver.

The Clowns were not very impressed by Hank. But after they started him at shortstop in a doubleheader against the Kansas City Monarchs, they began treating their rookie with a little more respect. He greeted the challenge of his first time at bat in a pro league by hitting a home run over the left-field fence. Then he rapped out a single and two doubles. By the end of the day, he had gotten 10 hits in 11 tries.

In spite of Hank's success, the Clowns felt they had to make an adjustment in his batting style. They didn't want him hitting cross-handed. So owner Syd Pollock converted Aaron to the standard grip—or so he thought. "I wasn't completely converted," says Aaron. "If I got two strikes on me and my back was to the dugout so they couldn't see me, I'd sneak my left hand up on top."

But no matter how he placed his hands, the results were the same—Henry Aaron hit baseballs very hard and very often. After 15 games, he was leading the Negro American League with a .467 average. And his exploits had not gone unnoticed.

Both the Braves and the Giants wanted to sign him, and they tried to outbid one another. The Braves won—by offering him $100 more. The Braves also told him they would start him in a low classification so that the pressure on him would be negligible.

He signed for $350 a month and immediately confronted the most frightening experience of his brief career. He had to *fly* from Charlotte, North Carolina, to the home of his new team in the Class-C Northern League in Eau Claire, Wisconsin. It was Aaron's first airplane ride and he will never forget it. "I rode that plane like it was a bronco," he says. "I was shaking and trying not to throw up all the way to Wisconsin."

Once he got his feet on the ground—and a bat in his hands—Aaron regained his confidence. He assaulted the Northern League pitchers with a barrage of base hits and within two weeks he was named to the league's All-Star team as a shortstop. In 87 games that season, he batted .336.

In 1953 he had to work harder because the Braves had stepped him up to faster company—the Class-A Jacksonville, Florida, club. Hank learned a great deal of baseball in Jacksonville. His manager, Ben Geraghty, constantly challenged him to play better. Geraghty never told him how good he was. He goaded Aaron on by telling him how good he *could* be. He made Hank a student of the game and cautioned him to learn from his mistakes.

One day Aaron stole second base three times. But each time the second baseman kept the ball instead of tossing it back to the pitcher, and each time he caught Hank taking his lead. After the game Geraghty tongue-lashed Aaron for his carelessness, and Hank has never forgotten the lesson.

He wound up the season with a .362 batting average, 125 RBIs and the Sally League's Most Valuable Player Award. He calls Geraghty "the best manager I ever played for."

The next season, at age 20, Hank Aaron became a major leaguer. He went to the Braves' spring training camp at Bradenton, Florida, to try out for the outfield job left open when Bobby Thomson broke his leg. The next thing he knew, he was standing at the plate in an exhibition game. Philadelphia's ace left-hander, Curt Simmons, was staring down at him from the mound. Not intimidated, Hank cracked a homer and a triple off Simmons and on opening day he was still in the line-up—and still hitting the best pitchers in the league. He had won the outfield job.

He hit .280 in his rookie year and was on his way to superstardom. The next year he hit .314 and played in his first All-Star Game. The fans voted for the starting All-Star teams in those days and had overlooked Aaron. But manager Leo Durocher picked Aaron as an alternate outfielder, and Hank's performance supported Leo's choice. Aaron hit two for two and drove in the tying run as the National League won on Stan Musial's homer in the twelfth inning. The next year, young Hank won the league batting title with a .328 mark.

Pitchers were learning to dread the sight of number 44 taking his stance in the right-handed batter's box. Hank drove the Dodgers' Don Newcombe into a frenzy one afternoon in Milwaukee. Big Newk, one of the league's top pitchers, had started Hank out with a blazing fast ball and Aaron smacked it for a double. On his next time up, Aaron lined out to center field. Newcombe slipped two strikes over on Hank when he came to bat for the third time. Then Don craftily threw a waste pitch, low and away. Hank leaned out and hit it like a golf ball into right-center field for another double. He was brushing off the dirt from the slide to second when he saw the angry Newcombe bearing down on him. Don stopped a foot away from Aaron. "Next time," shouted Newcombe, "I'm going to throw that thing *under* the plate to you. See if you can hit *that!*" Then Newk wheeled and stomped back to the mound. Aaron stood on second base and enjoyed a good laugh.

He got another laugh in a game against the Pirates. Bobby Bragan, who later became the Braves' manager, was then running the Pittsburgh club. He ordered Vernon Law to throw Aaron his knuckle ball on the first pitch. "Let's see what he can do with that for a start," Bragan said.

Law nodded, although he preferred to throw the knuckler only when ahead of the batters. In came the pitch and Hank went after it. As the ball sailed over the left-field fence for a home run, Bragan turned to reserves in the Pittsburgh dugout and moaned, "What's the use? No matter what you throw, that guy will hit it."

By 1966, Aaron was still feared as much as at any time in his career. The Dodgers' Sandy Koufax has said, "He's the last guy I want to see coming up. You don't get away with a mistake to Henry."

It is not just instinct that makes Aaron the hitter he is. Of course, he has the powerful wrists and quick reflexes that enable him to wait until the last second before bringing the bat around. But, more importantly, he is a crafty hitter who works at his trade. He tries to lull pitchers into mistakes. Occasionally, he will see a curve breaking into the dirt and he will swing and miss intentionally. He knows the pitcher will try to throw the same pitch for a strike later on—and he looks for that pitch.

Aaron remembers each pitch he hits for a homer —what kind of delivery it was and where it was thrown. Someone once mentioned a homer he had hit off Dodger Ron Perranoski in 1966, and Aaron nodded. "It was a fast ball, high and away," he said. "It was the first pitch and I guess I was looking for it. I figured he'd try to set me up for the sinker."

Baseball, according to Aaron, is a thinking game. "I have to study this game all the time," he says.

Aaron's style itself is unique. "Most guys," he says, "couldn't hit the way I do. I'm fortunate that all the things you have to do in baseball come naturally to me. I do have a hitch in my swing, and I hit off the front foot. I've seen the movies. The weight is forward, but you notice the hands are always back. If they throw me a change up, I'm not out front. I can adjust."

One day early in his career, Aaron came into Cincinnati and read in the papers that the Reds' pitchers were saying that they had found out how to stop him. They said they had discovered a flaw in his swing. Aaron was in a slump at the time, but he responded to the challenge with characteristic vigor. The teams played a double-header and Hank hit three home runs, three doubles, and a single.

Hank's relaxed, effortless style sometimes leaves people with the mistaken impression that he is indifferent to the action on the ball field.

"I know they think I don't care," he says, "I look like I'm running easy to first base, but I'm watching the outfielder and if necessary I can accelerate—I have the speed to shift gears."

As an outfielder, Aaron gets occasional criticism, too, for not sprinting after foul flies that twist into the stands Most players track the ball to the edge of the stands before giving up. "I know when the ball's going into the stands," Hank says. "What would it prove to run over there? That's false hustle. I hustle when I have to."

Hank's quiet effectiveness tends to obscure the fact that he's a superb all-round ballplayer. He has excellent speed and uses it to advantage on the base paths. He will take the extra base on hits to the outfield and he can steal when the team needs it. Aaron once stole 31 bases in a season. One of his teammates, Gene Oliver, has said that Hank could steal 100 if the team really needed them.

Defensively, Aaron possesses all the right equipment. He has wide range in the outfield and throws well. "If you need a shoestring catch, he'll make it,"

Hank slides into third and discovers he's safe; the third baseman has dropped the ball.

says former Brave manager Bobby Bragan. "He does it like Joe DiMaggio."

Aaron does not have the flamboyance of San Francisco's Willie Mays and is often underrated in departments other than hitting. But flashy or not, Hank does the job—and he does it with finesse.

Aaron has come a long way as a ballplayer and he has matured as a person as well. While he was playing in Jacksonville, he met the attractive Barbara Lucas and they were married before he left for Milwaukee. He has also invested his baseball earnings in a real estate business. And he is no longer frightened at the prospect of making a public speech.

But it is as a baseball player, of course, that Aaron has made his mark. One day Dodger manager Walter Alston was describing Aaron's skill. Alston told how his pitcher in a particular game had fired high and tight to brush Aaron back and had also thrown into the dirt to make him chase bad pitches. When Aaron was on base, the Dodgers tried every trick to pick him off. They roughed him up when he slid and slapped him hard with their tags.

"So he winds up," says Alston, "with two singles and a home run. He stole a base, robbed us of a triple with a great catch, accounted for four runs, and beat us from here to Toledo."

That's what happens when you challenge Hank Aaron, the natural. "More than anyone else," Alston has said, "Aaron has made me wish I wasn't a manager." Aaron could be paid no higher compliment than that.

Al Kaline 7

In 1955 Al Kaline hit .340 to lead the American League in hitting. Every ballplayer dreams of this kind of season. But Kaline's performance was even more remarkable because he was just 20 years old—the youngest player ever to win a major league batting title. For Tiger fans, who had not had a pennant winner in ten years, the future finally looked bright. They could hardly wait to see what Kaline was capable of once he acquired more experience.

Amid all the glowing predictions, however, came a word of caution from Hall of Famer Mel Ott, a former boy wonder himself. Ott had broadcast all the Tiger games in 1955 and he too had been impressed by Kaline's achievements that season.

"I never saw a kid who could do so many things as well as Kaline," Ott said early in 1956.

But Ott could not help wondering if the same thing that had happened to him might not happen to Kaline, too. "I had the best year I ever had when I was 21," said Ott. "I don't mean I didn't have any good seasons after that. I just never had another one *that* good. It might be the same way with Kaline. I can't explain why it happened to me the way it did, unless it's because I was young and full of vinegar. Maybe the pitchers got a little more careful with me after that."

Ott, who died in an automobile crash a few years later, never realized how accurate his words about Kaline would be. Year after year Kaline has worked hard trying to recapture the magic of 1955. Twice he has come close, hitting .327 in 1959, and .324 in 1961. But the 1955 season probably always will be his greatest.

In a sense, that season has also been Kaline's greatest burden. Since he has never again hit .340, many people feel he has not lived up to his vast potential. They have been waiting so intently for another Kaline explosion that they have been blinded to Kaline's steady performance year in and year out.

Kaline is the kind of ballplayer who is appreciated more by other baseball people than by the average fan. Every year *Sport* Magazine takes a confidential preseason poll of the major league players to determine who they feel will lead the two leagues in the individual categories. Invariably, a strong percentage of players picks Kaline to lead the league in hitting.

Strangely, Kaline had won only one batting title by the end of the 1966 season, yet he had had seven seasons in which he hit .304 or better. The ballplayers clearly feel that a fellow as consistent as Kaline is a threat to lead the league any year.

Kaline has had many managers in Detroit, and every one of them has been impressed by his ability. In 1955 Bucky Harris called him the finest young hitter he had ever seen. After Kaline had played only five seasons in the majors, Manager Jack Tighe said he was a cinch for the Hall of Fame. Bob Scheffing called him the best player he had ever managed. "I wouldn't trade him for Mantle *or* Mays," said Scheffing. And Charlie Dressen, who died recently, called Kaline a better all-round player than Jackie Robinson or Hank Aaron.

The late Fred Hutchinson, another ex-Detroit manager, grew very angry in 1962 when someone suggested that Kaline had not become a good right fielder until the Tigers had obtained center fielder Bill Bruton from Milwaukee.

"No one made a good outfielder out of Kaline!" said Hutch, practically shouting. "He is just the best right fielder in the business and he has been since he was 18 years old. He throws to the right base all the time and he never misses the relay man with a throw. That boy never made a mistake playing the outfield."

Hutch, of course, was exaggerating a little when he said Kaline never made a fielding mistake. What he meant to say was that, when Kaline does goof, his trigger reflexes and rifle-like arm usually bail him out. In a 1954 game against Cleveland, Kaline tried for a diving catch of a low line drive. He missed and Dale Mitchell, the hitter, headed for second. Still sprawled on the ground, Kaline grabbed behind him for the ball. He knew he had no time to get up and throw, so he threw to second while sitting down. Mitchell was out.

Kaline's all-out efforts in the field show that he is a team man first and an individual second. He knows that a hustling fielding play seldom shows up

Right fielder Al Kaline makes a spectacular catch against the Yankees.

in the box score, but he also knows that it can make the difference between winning and losing.

To Kaline, winning is what counts. That is why he has not tried to become a power hitter, even though the fans would much rather see a homer than a single. Kaline insists on taking his home runs as they come and he is as consistent in that department as he is in his batting average. From 1955 through 1966 he never hit fewer than 15 home runs a season nor more than 29.

"Sometimes I get mad because people are always looking for the home run instead of a good hit-and-run play, a good sacrifice or a good fielding play," Kaline has said. "I think the home run has made the game a lot less interesting than it used to be."

There is little doubt that Kaline could hit more home runs if he wanted to. He is solidly built at 6 feet 2 inches, and weighs 185 pounds. In fact, he was leading the league in homers in 1962, until he was disabled by an injury for two months. He finished the year with 29 home runs despite missing more than a third of the season. "I'm certain I could have hit 35 or 40 if I'd tried to," he said in 1963. But if I go for homers it throws the rest of my hitting off and I don't think I help the rest of the team as much as when I'm swinging away for base hits."

Kaline has often been called the perfect player. There are good reasons for this. He has demonstrated a mastery of every phase of the game, including base running. He stole 19 bases in 1960, and he has a total of more than 100 stolen bases for his career. The fact that Kaline is almost a cripple makes his stolen-base record even more remarkable.

When he was ten years old he suffered a bone disease in his left foot—the same disease Mickey Mantle had. Some of Al's bones were decayed and doctors had to operate on him three times. He was playing ball again when he was eleven and refused to worry about the foot, even though two of his toes could not touch the ground. Kaline learned to live with the deformity and ignored the occasional pain it gave him. But early in 1965 he noticed a large lump on the bottom of his left foot. Al's doctor gave him a pair of corrective shoes, which were hard to get used to. "At first," said Kaline, "I felt as though I was walking on marbles."

Kaline's foot bothered him during the rest of the 1965 season, and he was forced to sit out a game every once in a while. Unbelievably, a few critics thought he was faking. "Here we're trying to win the pennant and it sounds like I'm taking a rest," said Al. "The reason I don't play is because I can't play. My foot just can't take the pounding of a double-header. If I did play that second game, I'd be no good the next day . . . or I could be out longer than that."

The pain continued into the 1966 season, and Al was bothered during spring training by the hard Florida playing fields. But as the season wore on, the corrective shoes began to work, and he felt that his foot troubles were finally over.

Kaline's fans certainly hoped so, because in addition to foot trouble, he has always had enough other injuries to supply a dozen ordinary players. It is typical of Kaline that most of them could have been avoided if he had not tried to perform the impossible.

Injuries began hindering Al right from his first full season with the Tigers, in 1954. Toward the end of that season he had a hot streak and was on his way to a .300 average. He went 9 for 11 over a two-game period and his average was up to .286. Then he ran into a wall while chasing a fly. He caught the ball all right, but wound up in the hospital for five days. When he got out, he had lost his momentum and ended the season with a .276 mark.

In 1959 the Tigers learned what it means to have

A determined Kaline falls into the stands—after snaring a liner and tossing it back onto the field.

Kaline out of the line-up. They were within reach of first place in June when Al's cheekbone was caved in by a throw. While Al recuperated, the Tigers lost ground and fell out of the race.

Kaline was free of injuries for the next two years, but Manager Bob Scheffing could not understand why. Time after time, Scheffing would watch his star dive over the wire screens that were in front of the outfield wall at Tiger Stadium. Scheffing did not want to take any chances with Kaline and at the end of the 1961 season he removed the wire screens. "I don't want Al to kill himself," said the manager. "He's a ballplayer who never gives up."

But if Kaline could not stop a home run by crashing into the wire screens, he could find other ways to win ball games and practically destroy himself, all at the same time.

In 1962 Al made the best start of his career. By late May he was hitting .336 and leading the league with 13 home runs and 38 runs-batted-in. Then came a game against the Yankees on May 26. In the bottom of the ninth, two Yankees were out and the Tigers led, 2–1. Yankee catcher Elston Howard hit a little fly to short right field and Kaline raced in for the ball. Letting his reflexes take over, he hit the ground and snared the ball inches above the

The Tigers' prized right fielder hits the ground while making the costly catch that put him out of action for two months.

grass. The game was over, but the Tigers could only stare in horror as Kaline lay motionless. First baseman Norm Cash ran out and Kaline told him to get the trainer. Al knew right away something was wrong. He had hit the ground with the front of his shoulder instead of the back, and the impact had broken his collarbone. He was sidelined for two months. He finished the season with a respectable .304 batting average, but it was a disappointment for what had promised to be his finest season ever.

In 1963 Al was off again to a great start. And once more he ran into trouble when he put his desire to excel ahead of his personal safety. In late May he slammed into the Los Angeles outfield wall while trying in vain to stop a home run. His right knee took the brunt of the impact. The knee was gimpy for a while and sometimes it buckled when Al put pressure on it. Still, he continued to play and by the beginning of September he was in a duel for the batting title with Boston's Carl Yastrzemski. But then Al's knee really began to hurt and he thought he would need an operation. It was useless for him to try and continue playing. He favored the knee at the plate and this threw his timing off.

Kaline sat out the last two weeks of the season, coming off the bench just once to hit his 100th RBI.

He wound up with one to spare when, in a game against Minnesota, he hit a single, a triple and two home runs. Kaline's batting average was .312, but he lost the batting title by nine percentage points. Characteristically, he refused to blame it on his knee. But people who saw him play know better.

"Desire" has always been the key word behind Kaline's success. It's not surprising, because Al comes from a family where baseball was a way of life. He was born in Baltimore, Maryland, on December 19, 1934. And his father, as well as one grandfather and two uncles, were all semi-pro catchers. Al's father, Nicholas, a broommaker by trade, taught Al to pitch and Al did well in neighborhood games. But his pitching career ended quickly when he reported to the baseball team at Southern High School as a 130-pound freshman pitcher. He was cut from the squad. Then he tried second base, but was unsuccessful there, too. However, the coach at Southern liked Al's long and accurate throwing, and shifted him to the outfield. "That was the best break I ever got," Al says.

Perhaps Al's next best break occurred even before he entered high school. Charlie Johnson, a neighbor, had just been signed by Tiger scout Ed

Katalinas and he told the scout about another prospect. "I think you should keep an eye on a kid who lives just around the corner from here," Charlie told the scout. "His name is Al Kaline. He's only 15 now, but someday he'll be a great ballplayer."

Katalinas kept a constant watch over Kaline and during those four high school years saw him bat .427, make circus catches in the outfield and steal 48 bases. Kaline's base running was especially impressive. Sometimes he stole second and third on successive pitches. In one game he had been making considerable trouble for a young, confused catcher. When Al got on base again and was beginning to edge off first, a fan yelled some good advice to the catcher: "Throw to *third* and head him off!"

By the time Al was ready to graduate, nearly every major league club had expressed an interest in him. But when Al let it be known that he wanted a bonus, everyone except the Phillies, the Cardinals and the Tigers dropped out of the bidding. Al leaned toward the Tigers because of the interest shown by Katalinas. The question, though, was whether or not the Tigers were interested in Kaline, since it would take about $40,000 to get him.

To verify Katalinas' glowing reports, farm director John McHale went to Baltimore for a first-hand look. "What impressed me most in the games I saw him play," McHale said later, "was that every time you needed something done, Kaline would do it. In every clutch situation, he seemed to be in there. On top of that, his love for the game was something you could almost see."

Kaline and the Tigers came to terms and the first things Al did with the $40,000 were to pay off the mortgage on his parents' home and finance an operation for his mother. To Al, it was the least he could do to thank them for the encouragement they had given him in baseball.

Al went directly to the Tigers after he signed and played 30 games in the 1953 season. The next year he was a 19-year-old regular. He felt so secure in his job that he married his high school sweetheart, Louise Hamilton, at the end of the season.

Then came 1955, the year Kaline could do nothing wrong and the year he became the most talked-about player in the majors. "He always threw to the right base," said Mel Ott. "He was a smart outfielder. He ran the bases well. He just never quit hitting. He was alive out on the field, and he made you notice him, just the way he moved around."

Kaline made it all look so simple that people took his feats for granted. Al does not get annoyed

Rookie Al Kaline in 1953.

easily, but being taken for granted disturbs him. "All I've ever heard since I've been in baseball is that I make the game look easy," Al said in 1964. "Well, it hasn't been as easy as people think. Hitting is hard for me. They think all I have to do is go up to the plate and I'll automatically hit .300. I don't have that kind of ability. It may not look it, but I have to work hard for my hits."

With an attitude like that, it is not surprising that Kaline has never been too unhappy for failing to hit .340 again. He has always been so self-critical that his occasional shortcomings don't surprise him. "To be honest about it," he has said, "I felt that it was my fielding and not my hitting which kept me in the majors in those early years."

If Kaline learned anything from his 1955 season, it was the fact that a player has not proved anything until he shows what he can do *after* a spectacular season. "That's why," says Al, "I tell some of the guys on our club who have good years, 'Fine— you've had a good year. Now comes the tough part. You've got to work hard to stay up there.'" Other players might resent a statement like that if it came from a player without the record to back it up. But Kaline knows what he is talking about. He has never stopped working, and his record proves it.

Tony Oliva 8

At the age of 19 Pedro Oliva found himself alone in a strange country—the United States. He had no money, spoke no English and was more than just a little bit frightened. He wanted to go home, but a revolution was raging in Cuba. He couldn't get an airplane that would take him back to his homeland.

Pedro had come to America to play professional baseball with the Minnesota Twins. A scout for the Minnesota team, Joe Cambria, had seen him playing in Cuba in the province of Pinar Del Rio. Impressed by the youth's hitting, Cambria had told Pedro's father that he would like to take Pedro to America to play baseball for money.

Pedro had not wanted to go. He disliked the idea of leaving his mother and father and nine brothers and sisters, but his father told him that he must take advantage of the offer. "In America," he said, "you will play baseball every day and you will become rich and famous."

Actually Pedro had already been playing ball for almost as long as he could remember. Every Sunday he would go with his father, his four brothers and some neighbors to a vacant lot near the Oliva farm and play baseball. From Monday to Saturday they worked, but on Sunday they always played their favorite sport.

Pedro's father, a former semi-professional player, had shown him how to stand at bat, with his knees bent over and his body curled so that he could see the ball well. Over and over he urged the boy to be aggressive. "Hit the ball if you like it—no matter where it is," he said. "If you hit the ball hard and you are lucky, nobody will catch it."

One day Pedro's father was umpiring while Pedro batted. A pitch came in as high as the boy's head, and he didn't swing. When his father called out, "Strike!" the other players laughed. But his father justified his call by saying, "If you can reach the ball, you can hit it."

Pedro learned his lessons well. He became the best hitter in all of Pinar Del Rio, and eventually found himself on a plane en route for the United States with 20 other potential ballplayers. The plane landed at Miami Beach, Florida, and the young men climbed off, waiting to be checked out by a United States customs officer. When Pedro reached the head of the line, he handed the officer his visa. The man looked at it and said, "Tony Oliva, si?"

Pedro was startled when he heard the name. Then he suddenly remembered that when he had been packing to leave home he couldn't find his birth certificate anywhere. Because there had been no time to search for it, he took the one that belonged to his brother Tony, who was four years his senior.

"Si," Pedro finally answered the customs man. "Tony Oliva."

After the 21 young Cubans had gone through customs, Joe Cambria took them to Fernandena Beach, where the Minnesota Twins had their minor league camp. They arrived there just four days before the end of spring training. "Tony," as he was now known, received a team uniform and was allowed to play in three games. He got seven hits in ten tries. But on the fourth day Cambria told him that the Twins had decided they couldn't use him. They had filled all their minor league rosters and there was no room left.

So 19-year-old Tony Oliva was stranded in a foreign country, far from his family and the farm where he had grown up. Since he couldn't return to Cuba, he went with two of his friends to Charlotte, North Carolina, where another friend was playing ball on a Minnesota farm team.

At Charlotte his friend arranged for Tony to work out with the team. Oliva's long, lean frame, his quick wrists, his unharnessed power and the way he slashed at the ball impressed Paul Howser, general manager of the Charlotte club. He picked up the telephone and called Minnesota, advising the Twins to sign this boy called Tony Oliva.

Within one month Oliva had been signed, released and signed again by the same team. It's not often that a player gets a second chance to sign a baseball contract with a team like the Minnesota Twins.

The Twins assigned Oliva to Wytheville, Virginia, in the Appalachian League. When he arrived, the season was almost one-third over, but he played in 64 games and led the league in hitting with a remarkable .410 average. He also led in hits, with a total of 102, and in RBIs with 81. At the same time he tallied up the most errors by an outfielder, making 14 in 96 chances for an .854 fielding average, one of the lowest ever recorded anywhere.

The Twins sent him to play winter ball in Puerto Rico. They thought that the additional experience would help him to tighten up on his fielding. Also, he would be hitting against more experienced pitching. Although Oliva batted .365, he lost the Puerto Rican batting title to Orlando Cepeda, who hit .368.

Tony Oliva seemed too good to be believed. For the 1962 season the Twins sent him back to Charlotte —this time to play, not to visit. His hitting continued to be excellent, and his fielding improved tremendously. He batted .350, missing the championship by only two points, and he had 17 home runs and 93 runs-batted-in. By now Oliva was being talked about throughout the baseball world.

After he finished at Charlotte, the Twins called him up for the last two weeks of the season. In nine games, Tony batted .444 and his reputation continued to grow. He was considered one of the hottest prospects in the game, although there was one disturbing thing about him. According to his birth certificate, Tony Oliva was 26 years old. The professionals considered this very old for a rookie. Still, he swung a great bat, and during his brief stay in Minnesota he became the center of attention. Reporters wrote about the Cuban farm boy who spoke no English, but swung a bat like Ted Williams.

Finally one reporter, who was interviewing Oliva through an interpreter, discovered that he was not Tony Oliva, aged 26, but Pedro Oliva, 22. The reporter asked why he kept on using his brother's name.

"I am hitting good as Tony Oliva," the young Cuban explained. "Why should I change?"

In the spring of 1963 Tony was invited to take spring training with the Twins. The team managers hoped he could make the team and fill their need for a left-handed power hitter to counterbalance their right-handed sluggers, Harmon Killebrew and Bob Allison. They put Oliva into the hands of Zoilo Versalles, their likable, experienced Cuban shortstop. Versalles' job was to take Oliva with him, serve as his interpreter and generally help to make him feel at home. Soon Versalles became convinced that Oliva would someday make the Hall of Fame. He even went so far as to tell a visitor to the Twins' camp that Oliva was the new Ty Cobb.

"What makes you say that?" asked the visitor.

"Whoever can hit for high average, whoever can run, whoever can throw, he is the new Ty Cobb," Versalles replied. "Oliva is Ty Cobb."

But when the season opened, Oliva was at Dallas-Fort Worth in the Texas League, where it was hoped he would pick up some extra polish. Suddenly he seemed far removed from the legendary Ty Cobb. In fact, he wasn't even the old Tony Oliva any more. Disappointed and disillusioned, he got off to an extremely slow start. By June he was hitting just .235, and the fans had begun to ridicule him. But he got the tonic he needed on a 15-day road trip. He went on a batting binge and returned with a .288 average.

The home fans started cheering, and Oliva finished the season with a .304 mark, just four points below the league leader. He hit 23 home runs and tallied 74 RBIs. At last the Twins were convinced he was ready for the big leagues.

And ready he was. Manager Sam Mele moved Allison in from the outfield, putting him on first base. He put the veteran first baseman, Vic Power, on the bench. And he made Tony Oliva his regular right fielder.

Tony started 1964 as if he was back on the vacant

Right fielder Tony Oliva in action.

lot in Pinar Del Rio. By the end of May he was batting over .380. Pitchers went wild trying to figure a way to pitch him. If they threw outside he drove the ball to left. If they threw inside he pulled the ball hard to right. If they threw high he went up and got it, and if they threw low he went down after it. His tremendous power forced the infield to play back, and his great speed helped him to beat out slow rollers and bunts.

As he faced the big league pitchers, he seemed to be following the advice his father had given him so many times. "If you can reach the ball, you can hit it. If you hit the ball hard and you are lucky, they will not catch it."

When Oliva went into a mid-season slump, he didn't panic, nor did he alibi. "I am not lucky," he said. "I am hitting the ball hard, but they are catching it. Soon I will be lucky again and they will not catch it."

He had his biggest day on May 7, 1964. Against the Los Angeles Angels, he had two singles and two home runs (one a grand slam) and drove in six runs in a 9–1 victory. By the time the season ended, he led the American League in hitting, with a .323 average. He also had 32 home runs, 94 RBIs and was the first rookie in the history of the American

League to win a batting title. Naturally he was a unanimous selection for American League Rookie of the Year.

He should have been enormously pleased with his success, but Oliva was unable to enjoy it fully, for he couldn't share his triumph with his family. His father's letters told of his pride, but Tony continued to feel lonely. He was homesick. He missed his family and longed to be with them. Although he was a baseball hero, he had no home to call his own.

When the American League season ended, Oliva flew off to Puerto Rico to play winter ball. The season there lasted right up until it was time to report to the Twins for spring training. Wherever he went he took along five suitcases, which carried his entire belongings—his clothes, his record player and the baseball he hit for his first major league, grand-slam home run off Dan Osinski of the Angels.

As the 1965 season got under way, Tony never lost stride. He kept right on swinging. Then in May he injured the middle finger of his right hand while sliding into second, and his hitting began to fall off. By June he was hitting below .250, and the experts had practically counted him out of the race for his second consecutive batting title.

The doctors advised an operation, but Oliva re-

Wearing a glove to protect the injured middle finger of his right hand, Tony swats another home run.

sisted. The Twins were in the thick of the fight for the American League pennant, and he knew that even half an Oliva was better than none. He not only refused the operation, but even refused to take time off to let his injured finger heal.

"If I take one or two days' rest, it does not help," he argued. "You must take four or five days. But if I take four or five days, I will lose my timing and I will not hit. So it is better not to rest. It is better to play every day."

The pain became so acute that Oliva was practically hitting with one hand. But because he knew the Twins needed him, he managed to forget the pain and slam the ball out in the way that people had come to expect.

On July 21 he collected five hits against Boston. Exactly one week later he had five singles against Washington. On August 8 he added three singles and a double against Washington. The Twins were moving now and so was Tony Oliva. By September he had pulled his average up to .290, and the Twins were driving to the top of the league.

In the middle of September the Twins went to Chicago to meet the second-place White Sox in a vital two-game series. In the first game Tony had a typical Oliva day. The first time he singled up the

Oliva celebrates with teammates Jim Kaat and Bob Allison after the Twins beat the Dodgers in the second game of the 1965 World Series.

middle; the second time he singled to right. The third time he doubled to left. The Twins won the game, 3–2.

"That kid," Manager Sam Mele said admiringly, "could hit wearing boxing gloves."

The Twins won the second game, too, and pulled away from the rest of the league to win their first American League pennant. The race was over for the Twins, but not for Oliva. He didn't stop hitting. He continued his surge and finished with a .321 average to become the first player to win two consecutive batting championships in the American League since Ted Williams did it in 1957–58.

The last American Leaguer to win three consecutive batting titles was Ty Cobb. As Tony Oliva entered his third major league season in 1966, he had a chance to make a prophet out of Zoilo Versalles. On May 13 he slammed two singles, a double and triple against the Washington Senators. It was the fifth time in his big league career that he had four hits in one game. By May 16 he was leading the league with a .391 average.

Then he began to dive.

During August he experienced the worst slump of his career, tumbling below the .300 mark for the first time all season. Apparently 1966 was to be his

The Twins' slugger from Cuba takes off after slamming out another liner.

most frustrating year. His finger hurt him and he injured his thigh. An abscessed tooth left him with a painful and swollen jaw, and he was unable to get rid of a cold he picked up in Los Angeles. Although he suffered through a dreadful slump, with only five hits in 24 at-bats, he played in spite of his cold. Then he tried resting for two days, but that didn't help.

On August 16 a doctor in Minnesota advised Oliva not to play. He played anyway. In the seventh inning he told pitcher Camilo Pascual, "I don't think I can make it." Then he went to bat and hit a game-winning home run.

Oliva pulled his average back up to .323 and was leading the league by the time the Twins went to Boston. Then he fell apart again. He made only five hits in his next 41 times at bat, and in one game he struck out three times—the first time that had happened in his major league career.

But to Oliva's credit, even though his hitting slumped, his fielding did not falter. The young fielder who had made such a poor showing in Wytheville became a pro in Minnesota. When he wasn't winning games with his bat, he was winning them with his glove and arm. He didn't brood in the outfield after he failed to hit at bat.

In a game against Cleveland, he threw out speedy Chico Salmon with a bullet throw from deep right field all the way to home on the fly. Salmon was trying to score from second on a single with the tying run. Catcher Jerry Zimmerman caught the ball waist high.

"Tomorrow," said pitching coach Johnny Sain, "we're going to have Oliva pitch batting practice from right field."

With Frank Robinson, a fugitive from the National League, leading the Baltimore Orioles to the 1966 pennant with his bat, Tony Oliva's reign as American League batting champion came to an end. Robinson won the batting title with a .316 average, spoiling Oliva's bid for a third consecutive crown. But despite his slump, Oliva finished second with .307. No other American Leaguer batted .300. That, however, was of little consolation to Oliva. He felt he had made a dismal showing and was determined to make up for it in 1967.

Perhaps that is the greatest compliment that can be paid to Tony Oliva, a major league hero who keeps trying. He manages to hit .307 in a bad year!

Joe Torre   9

Joe Torre was 16 and weighed 240 pounds. He was fat, there was no denying that, but he was also the best baseball player in the neighborhood. His friends regarded him as something of a celebrity because his brother Frank played first base for the Milwaukee Braves and was the teammate of Eddie Mathews, Hank Aaron, Lou Burdette and Warren Spahn. Therefore, Joe always had major league baseballs, bats and gloves and he could tell exciting baseball stories to his friends.

Warren Spahn, one of the greatest left-handed pitchers of all time, was Joe's particular favorite.

Although Joe had never met Spahn, he followed the great pitcher's progress in the papers and he listened attentively whenever Frank spoke of him.

Joe's big moment came one day when the Braves were playing the Dodgers in Brooklyn (the Dodgers had not yet moved to Los Angeles). Frank had promised to take him to the ball park and introduce him to the players. Joe had looked forward to the event for weeks, going over in his mind the things he might say to his heroes:

"I hope you hit three home runs today, Eddie."

"You pitched a terrific game against the Phillies last week, Lou."

Above all, he would meet the famous Spahn. He would have plenty of exciting stories to bring back to his friends.

Finally, the big day arrived and there he was, standing in front of Spahn's locker and his brother was saying, "Warren, I'd like you to meet Joe, my big little brother."

"Boy are you fat!" said Spahn.

It was not really Joe's fault that he was so fat. As the youngest of five Torre children, he had been the baby whom everybody pampered and fed. "Eat, Joseph, eat," they would say. "Grow up big and strong."

When Joe was still 11, and Frank was playing in Denver, Joe and his mother, sister and cousin took a train from New York to visit him. They stayed a month and in that time Joe learned to eat like a major leaguer. He had huge breakfasts, double-thick steaks for dinner, then ate hot dogs, milk shakes and ice cream during the games. Later, he continued to eat like a big leaguer and, as a result, became the heaviest player on his school and neighborhood teams.

As he grew, Joe Torre thought only of becoming a major league baseball player someday. He played first and third base for a Brooklyn sandlot team called the Cadets and for his high school, St. Francis Preparatory. Whenever he played, he attracted many scouts. They were lured by his name and by stories of his unusual ability to hit a baseball into the great beyond.

The stories were true. The scouts who saw him were immediately impressed with Joe's hitting, but they were also skeptical. They sent back identical reports to their front offices: "Good bat, but too fat and too slow to be considered a prospect."

The one baseball man who refused to believe that Joe was not a big league prospect was brother Frank Torre. Nobody criticised Joe more for his eating than Frank, and nobody praised him more as a baseball player.

"I knew he had more ability than I ever dreamed of having," Frank said. "He always had all the tools and I'm not saying it just because he's my brother."

As a solution, Frank persuaded Joe to try catching. Joe's build and his inability to run, combined with the general shortage of hitting catchers, made the idea seem obvious. Also, catching was Joe's only salvation if he was determined to be a major league ballplayer.

Joe had graduated from high school in June, 1958, without so much as a tumble from a major league scout. He had been offered a baseball scholarship to St. John's University, but made no commitment because he still clung to the hope that he would catch some scout's eye.

Instead of going to college, Torre decided to work for a year. He secured a job on the floor of the American Stock Exchange in New York City, running messages and doing errands. In the spring he would be able to play ball for the Cadets. He had asked the Cadets' manager if he could catch, and the manager agreed to alternate him with another catcher.

By spring of 1960, when the Cadets began to play again, maturity, determination and his hectic job at the Stock Exchange had helped Joe to lose 15 pounds. But most major league scouts had already closed their books on him as a too-fat, too-slow third baseman. Fortunately, however, Joe was catching for the Cadets on the day that a veteran scout named Honey Russell was in the stands. Russell had scouted Joe as a third baseman, but he had never seen him catch before.

"I couldn't believe it when I first saw him," Russell says. "He was a natural. He had good hands, a fine arm and lots of poise for a kid who had just started catching. Even his hitting had improved. He seemed to be thinner through the chest and he was smooth and effortless behind the plate. There was never any question about his hitting."

Unsuccessful as a fat third baseman, Torre had suddenly become a valuable property as a catcher. Honey Russell paid a call on the Torre family and offered Joe a contract. With the scholarship to St. John's still in his pocket, Torre was in a good bargaining position. He managed to get a $20,000 bonus out of Russell.

After he signed the contract, Joe hustled off to the Braves' rookie camp in Florida. But the Braves' general manager, John McHale, took one look at him and decided that $20,000 was a very high price to pay for beef. He fired off a telegram of disapproval to Russell. Another club official, farm director John Mullen, was equally disturbed. "You're too fat," he said. "Lose some weight." A month later, Mullen returned to camp and took another look at Torre. Hard work in the hot Florida sun had turned Torre's flab into muscle. "That's better," said Mullen.

The Braves started Joe out at Eau Claire, Wisconsin, in the Class C Northern League. At Eau Claire he led the league in hitting with a .344 average, had 16 home runs and 74 RBIs and made only nine errors in 117 games.

In 1961 he was promoted to the Braves' top farm team, Louisville, in the class AAA American Association. After 27 games, Joe was hitting .342. But he did not stay in Louisville very long.

In Milwaukee, the Braves' manager, Charlie Dressen, was worried because his veteran catcher, Del Crandall, had developed a mysterious arm ailment and was unable to play. By May 20 Dressen had to do something about the situation. "Get me Torre," he demanded.

Louisville was playing in Omaha at the time, and

Joe was fast asleep when the telephone rang in his hotel room at 1:00 A.M. Louisville's manager, Ben Geraghty, told him that the Braves had called him up to the majors. This was exciting news for Joe. He caught a 3:30 A.M. flight to Chicago and from there, switched to a flight to Cincinnati. After traveling all morning, he reached Cincinnati at noon, tired but expectant. Dressen told him to take the afternoon off, because he would be catching a double-header the next day. The Braves' manager was wasting no time!

Torre caught both games, hit a single, a double and a homer and threw out three runners attempting to steal. It was a rather impressive debut.

But because he was a rookie, Torre still had to prove himself. Major league base runners wanted to find out how the 20-year-old catcher would stand up to the "clay-pigeon" play. This takes place when the catcher receives the ball from right field just as a runner comes flying in from third. Usually, the runner will try to break up the play by throwing himself into the catcher.

Early in the year Houston's Johnny Temple put Torre to the test three times. The first time, Temple hurtled into him head first and was tagged out. The second time, he hit Torre in the chest with his knees

Torre sprawls on the ground after a collision with Houston's Johnny Temple.

and ripped open his pants with his spikes. Joe dropped the ball. The third time, Temple put his foot in Torre's stomach, but Joe held the ball for the out. He proved that he could take the rough-and-tumble action of the major leagues.

That season Joe also experienced one of the biggest thrills of his baseball career. He was the catcher when his hero, Warren Spahn, won his 300th game. Spahn no longer joked about Torre's weight, he just praised Joe's talent. "From the very first day," Spahn said, "you knew this was an exceptional kid."

Torre caught 113 games in his rookie year, batted .278, with 10 home runs and 42 RBIs. But Crandall recovered in 1962, and had such an outstanding season that Torre could play in only 80 games. Still, Joe batted a respectable .282.

By 1963 Torre was doing most of the catching for the Braves. At the end of the season the team's front office traded Crandall to the Giants, and Torre moved in as first-string catcher. He responded by having his finest season. He batted .321 and became the first National League catcher in nine years to hit over .300. He also had 20 home runs and 109 RBIs. At the age of 23, Torre had become the outstanding all-around catcher in the league.

"Torre's not good," said the Braves' manager, Bobby Bragen, in the spring of 1966 (after the team had moved to Atlanta). "He's the best. The best at hitting. The best at throwing. The best at catching."

By midyear, Bragen had been replaced as manager by Billy Hitchcock. Torre's boss had changed, but the new boss's opinion of Torre was the same. Hitchcock felt that Torre had the chance to be one of the greatest catchers of all time.

Veteran manager and former catcher Birdie Tebbetts listed five things that a great player should be able to do: hit for bases, hit for distance, field, throw and run. He felt that although Torre was not a runner he made up for this lack with his other abilities.

Additional testimonies to Torre's abilities have come from the Pittsburgh Pirate manager, Harry Walker, and former catcher Joe Garagiola. Both feel that a manager could form a new team around Torre. In fact, George Weiss, president of the New York Mets, once offered John McHale half a million dollars for him in order to put some life into his cellar-bound club.

There is only one reservation ever mentioned when baseball people attempt to evaluate Joe Torre's greatness:

Joe crouches behind the plate.

"He's still so young," Tebbetts says. "He's got a long way to go before he can be rated with the Cochranes and Dickeys and Hartnetts and Berras. A lot could happen, but if he keeps going as he has been, he will rate with the best of them."

In 1953 Roy Campanella of the Brooklyn Dodgers set a record for catchers by hitting 41 home runs. In 1966, at age 26, Torre belted 36 home runs. And he is already attacking Yogi Berra's career record for home runs by a catcher. Yogi hit 358 homers in 17 seasons in baseball. By 1966 Torre had slugged 112 homers. And from 1964 through 1966 he averaged almost 30 a year. If he continues at that rate, he could top Campanella in career home runs in five seasons and pass Berra in nine.

As great as Torre's hitting has been—his lifetime batting average for six seasons in the major leagues is an even .300—his catching is the real surprise story. It is unusual for a young player, especially one who caught only about 50 games before he signed a professional contract, to become so adept at catching in such a short time.

Torre's baseball poise has contributed a great deal to his success. Hitchcock attributes his poise to the fact that, as a boy, Torre spent much of his time around ballplayers. "He wasn't awed the first

Left-hander Warren Spahn congratulates his catcher, Joe Torre, as they walk to the dugout after an impressive victory.

"One of baseball's most durable superstars."

time he walked into a major league clubhouse like most kids are," Billy points out. "Because his brother was a big leaguer, he knew how to handle himself."

Another factor in his success is his remarkable handling of pitchers. Joe is a steadying influence on a nervous pitcher. In a close game his confident instructions to the mound can mean the difference between winning and losing the game.

"All he has to do," says Garagiola, "is not shave and some kid pitcher out there looks in at that tough face behind the plate and he's more scared of Torre than he is of the hitter."

Torre himself feels that "the catcher is the only man in the park who can see everything that's happening just about every minute of the game. You're always in the game, you're thinking all the time. You're helping the pitcher, working with him, fighting his battles when the umpire gives him a bad call."

He is no longer Joe Torre, Frank's fat kid brother. He is Joe Torre, the best catcher in baseball, respected by all baseball people for his hitting, fielding and throwing. He has matured into a solid 210 pounds and has become one of baseball's most durable superstars while filling one of its most vital positions.

Brooks Robinson   10

Brooks Robinson of the Baltimore Orioles has a reputation for cool-headedness that is unrivaled by any other player in the game. In fact, the Orioles' great third baseman is often compared to a mechanical man because of his calm effectiveness in the infield.

For example, there is a play he made against the Minnesota Twins in 1963. The Twins' batter, Johnny Goryl, hit a scorching shot down the third baseline. Robinson dove to his right and backhanded the ball, but it skipped out of his glove. The impact spun him around so that his back was to first base. Instinctively he grabbed the ball and blindly threw across his body to first. Goryl was out by a scant half-step. The Minnesota player threw up his hands in frustration and disbelief.

It isn't so amazing that Robinson should have made such a play. Every third baseman has probably made a similar play. What's incredible about Robinson is the fact that he does it day in and day out, year after year. Such consistency is the true mark of the superstar. As additional proof of this consistency, if any is needed, he has won the American League's Golden Glove award for third basemen for seven years in a row.

Robinson makes plays look so easy that people tend to forget how difficult a third baseman's job can be. Although he may look perfectly relaxed, he knows he cannot ease up for a minute without risking disaster. He will always remember the time he let his mind wander in a game against Kansas City a few years ago.

During the first inning, instead of thinking about the hitter, Gino Cimoli, Robinson was worrying about his shoes. It was a logical concern, for he always has two pairs of baseball shoes and two gloves —one set of equipment for practice and one for the game. This day he had forgotten to change into his game shoes after practice, and he was wondering who would go into the clubhouse between innings and get them for him.

All of a sudden Cimoli bunted down the third baseline. It was a surprise play and Cimoli couldn't have picked a better moment for it, though of course he wasn't aware that Robinson was daydreaming. By the time Robinson snapped into action, he realized that the delay had cost him a precious fraction of a second. Nevertheless he tried to get Cimoli out, with a late, wild throw to first. It was his first error in 34 games.

Ever since then, Robinson has forced himself to concentrate. When that deep concentration is combined with his trigger-quick reflexes, the fans see one of the most spectacular third basemen in the history of baseball.

The Cimoli incident can be compared to another bunt situation that occurred during a game with the White Sox. He had moved up halfway to home plate—an extremely dangerous position to play if the hitter decides not to bunt at the last instant. That is exactly what Jim Landis chose to do. He swung viciously and the ball shot directly toward Robinson's head. The robot in Robinson took over. He caught the ball and threw it to the shortstop—before Landis even finished his swing.

Sometimes Robinson amazes his teammates as much as he amazes the fans and opposing players. Joe Pepitone of the Yankees once hit a bunt to the right of the mound. Oriole pitcher Stu Miller hadn't taken two steps off the mound before he had to duck to avoid Robinson's throw to first. "And I'm not slow," said Miller.

Another time Robinson ran full speed down the left-field line to catch a pop foul. He was so far out of position after making the catch that he threw to left-fielder Boog Powell, who was in a better spot to make the relay into the infield. But before Powell even had a chance to focus on the ball it smashed against his sunglasses, shattering one of the lenses. He was not harmed—just awed. "He did it so fast," said Powell, "I couldn't get my hands up."

Robinson's ability to appear calm and cool at third base stems from his self-assurance. He knows what he is doing and has faith that his body will react at the right moment. But he is just as calm in other situations, too, for it is not part of his nature to get ruffled. He has never been thrown out of a game, has never been fined by the league for misconduct and has never even thrown a temper tantrum.

Oriole third baseman Brooks Robinson makes a dazzling play, catching up with the ball in time to throw Yankee Bobby Richardson out at first.

Even when the situation calls for retaliation against an opposing player, Robinson can't bring himself to seek revenge. He prefers to score his points by winning ball games. In a game against the Yankees in 1962, he hit a home run off Ralph Terry. The next time Robinson came to bat, Terry threw a pitch behind Robinson's head, forcing him to hit the dirt. He got up quickly, brushed off his uniform and stepped back into the batter's box. He gave Terry no angry looks, uttered no threats. Instead, he appeared willing to believe that the pitch had been an accident. "Before the next game," says one Oriole, "Terry was hanging around the batting cage, wanting to apologize. Robbie made it easy for him. He shook the guy's hand. You know what he is? He's a darn saint. He can't hate *anybody*."

Brooks Robinson was born on May 18, 1937, in Little Rock, Arkansas. As a boy, Brooks rarely let pain and injuries bother him. In the second grade he broke his arm and then a while later he broke his collarbone, too. Each time he refused to cry. He was always happy, but never happier than when playing baseball. When he was 14 he had a newspaper route. One of his customers was the Hall of Fame catcher and ex-Yankee, Bill Dickey. "I'd toss his paper halfway over the roof," says Robinson, "hoping he was looking out and would see what an arm I had."

As a teenager, however, Brooks' throwing arm was not exceptional. Neither was his speed. Because of these two weaknesses, no major league team offered him more than $4,000, which was the largest bonus he could get and still be farmed out to a minor league team. So he had to decide whether he would accept the small bonus or take advantage of the athletic scholarships being offered by Arkansas University and other schools. He had made all-state in basketball and had run the 880 in track, so he was a fine prospective college athlete.

Brooks' father had been an outstanding amateur softball player and had been working with him from the time Brooks could walk. But he refused to influence his son's decision. He only pointed out how few minor league players make it to the majors. Young Brooks, though, felt he could leap over any hurdle and optimistically signed with the Orioles.

At 18, in his first pro season, he hit .331 in the Piedmont League. At the tail end of the 1955 season the Orioles brought him up to play in Baltimore. He was brought up at the end of the next two seasons as well. In 1958 he played the whole season in Baltimore. His fielding was splendid, but his hitting left much to be desired. He lacked power and his average in 1958 was just .238.

In 1959 Robinson was sent down to the minors once more—this time to Vancouver in the Pacific Coast League. Worse than that, a few days after arriving there, he had an accident that nearly finished his baseball career. While chasing a foul ball, he impaled his right upper forearm on the steel hook of a guard rail. The arm had to be cut loose and he was taken to the hospital. There, doctors debated whether the nerves and tendons had been cleanly cut or badly mangled. If they were mangled, Robinson would never be able to make the throw from third base again. While the doctors discussed the seriousness of the case, the unruffled third baseman joked with the nurses.

Fortunately the cut was clean and, after six weeks of pain and awkward throwing, Robinson was back in Baltimore—this time for good. He recovered so completely that he began hitting better than ever. Almost overnight he changed from a .240 hitter to a solid .280 hitter or better. The fans were so delighted to have him back that they gave him a standing ovation after he hit a little pop-up in his first time at bat. After that, Robinson knew that whatever his problems in baseball might be, the Baltimore fans would not be among them.

That season Robinson also knew that his bachelor days were numbered. While leaving Boston on a United Airlines flight one night, Robinson, who is not a very forward fellow, tried to make the attractive stewardess aware of his presence. "Watch out for these other guys," he said. "They're all married. I'm the only single man aboard." The stewardess became extremely aware of him—so much so that he and pretty Constance Butcher were married little more than a year later.

Somehow Robinson could not keep from getting injured again and again. One of his worst injuries occurred when he was chasing a foul ball near the seats in Detroit. For some unexplained reason the groundskeeper had hung a clothesline in foul territory. Robinson ran right into it, tripped and landed face first on a concrete ledge. He lay unconscious on the ground. When his teammates and trainer Ed Weidner reached him, they saw a fearful mess. His lower jaw had been laid open.

Finally Robinson opened his eyes.

"Do you know where you are?" asked Weidner, fearing a concussion. When Robinson did not answer, somebody said, "Call an ambulance."

That was too much for Robinson. He staggered to his feet. "What's the matter—didn't you ever see someone shook up?" he said. "Give me my glove and let's play ball."

They put a bandage on his jaw to hold it together and Robinson kept on playing. In the next inning, he hit a Don Mossi curve ball into right field to drive in the winning run. His teammates watch such performances with good-natured envy. Boog Powell says, "I sure wish I had what he's got."

Soon everything began to go so well for Robinson that his success seemed unreal to him. He hit .294 in 1960 and .287 in 1961. Then in 1962, he made a discovery that has helped him to become one of baseball's best players. During spring training in Florida that year, Robinson picked up another player's bat by accident. The bat was lighter and shorter than the one Robinson had been using and he found that his hands, instead of being three inches apart, as usual, gravitated naturally to the end of the short bat. In an exhibition game that day, he hit a home run over the center-field fence in the Miami stadium. The fence was 40 feet from home plate and more than 30 feet high. The bat felt good in his hands and Robinson used it the rest of the year. He wound up the season by hitting

.303, with 23 home runs and 86 runs-batted-in. However, the next season, 1963, turned out to be quite a disappointment for Oriole fans.

Brooks Robinson, the budding superstar, was one of the flops of the year. His average plummeted to .251, his home runs to 11 and his RBIs to 67. Sports writers asked which year represented the real Brooks Robinson—1962 or 1963? Even Brooks did not know for sure.

One concrete problem was Robinson's trouble with the high fast ball. He struck out 84 times in 1963. A normal strikeout total is about 55 times. He also played the season with infected tonsils and adenoids, which required surgery at the end of the year. His critics, however, looked for other reasons for his poor performance. They saw that he weighed two or three pounds more than his normal 185 pounds, so they said he was overweight. They also said he was spending too much time at his restaurant and his sporting-goods store.

Typically, Robinson refused to pay attention to the critics. When he went to spring training in 1964, he devoted his time to the real problem—the high fast ball. He worked hard on his batting and by opening day he had already made a great deal of improvement. In fact, he had improved so much that people were saying that he wasn't even the same ballplayer as the Brooks Robinson of 1962. Every time the Orioles needed a key play in the field, Robinson seemed to make it. Every time they needed a big hit, Robinson seemed to get it. The Orioles still had too many holes in their roster to win the pennant, but if any man deserved to be on a winning team, it was Robinson. He finished the season with personal highs in every major department: 28 home runs, 118 RBIs and a .317 batting average. He was the sure winner of the league's Most Valuable Player Award, the highest honor a player can receive.

Robinson was in big demand at banquets that winter, a pleasant switch from the dreary winter of the year before. The only thing he did not care for was receiving all the "comeback" awards that baseball organizations gave him. "I felt uncomfortable making a comeback at 27 years old," he said. But at 27, with ten years of pro ball behind him, Robinson had already had a noteworthy career.

As he moved into his mature years as a ballplayer, the future seemed clouded not by his own weaknesses but by those of his team. He wanted nothing more than to play in a World Series. In 1965 he had another fine year (hitting .297), but the Orioles fell short of their pennant hopes.

In 1966, however, the Baltimore team had an unexpected break—one that was to mean as much to them as acquiring Brooks Robinson. They added a second Robinson to the roster.

This one was named Frank. People were amazed when Baltimore was able to acquire the slugger from Cincinnati. They said that with Frank and Brooks batting third and fourth, the Orioles were sure to win the pennant. And that is exactly what happened. Brooks finally got his wish when Baltimore outclassed the rest of the league for the pennant and then swept the Dodgers in four straight games in the World Series.

The acquisition of Frank put Brooks in a new light. He was no longer the Orioles' single superstar, the only one they could depend on. Brooks adjusted by playing a less glamorous role, something the Orioles had not been able to afford before. He learned to sacrifice himself for the sake of a runner on base. Time and again, with Frank on second base, Brooks would deliberately hit behind him so that Frank could advance to third and be in position to score. For this reason Brooks was thrown out more often than might have been the case if he had taken his normal swing. But over the course of the season this unselfishness showed up in the number of games won by the Orioles.

To maintain, however, that Brooks Robinson was merely a sacrificial lamb in 1966 is completely false. He saved his biggest performances for the most important moments. In the first game of the World Series, he followed up Frank's first-inning homer with one of his own and set the pattern for the Oriole team's total domination of the Dodgers. Throughout the four games Brooks made sparkling plays in the field, including a crucial play in the fourth game that helped preserve a 1–0 Baltimore victory.

Perhaps the best of many shining hours for Brooks in 1966 came in the All-Star game in St. Louis. He got three of the American League's six hits, scored its only run, set an All-Star game record for third basemen with eight chances and took away three sure National League hits. For the first time in the five years during which a Most Valuable Player had been named for the All-Star game, sports writers selected a player from the losing team—Brooks Robinson.

Before Brooks Robinson came along, most people thought Pie Traynor was the greatest third baseman

High-flying Brooks Robinson leaps across the infield to congratulate Oriole pitcher Dave McNally after the final out in the final game of the 1966 World Series.

who ever lived. Now they're not so sure and the former superstar doesn't help one bit in settling the debate. "Robinson is wonderful on every type of play," Traynor says. "He's just the best there is."

Index

Page numbers in italics refer to photographs

Aaron, Hank, 92–109, 113, 147
   in All-Star game, 102–103
   batting of, 95, 97, 103–105
   childhood of, 97–99
   home runs of, 93–94, 95, 97, 105
   Most Valuable Player, 97
   photographs of, *92, 96, 107*
   in World Series, 95–97
Allen, Richie, 38
Allison, Bob, 61, 134, 135, *141*

All-Star games, 23, 102–103, 176
Alston, Walter, 39, 44, 50, 55, 108–109
American Association, 152
American League, 6, 7, 9, 15, 62, 111, 137–138, 140, 142, 145, 164, 176
Anderson, Wayne, 38
Antonelli, Johnny, 94
Appalachian League, 132

INDEX

Atlanta Braves, 93–94, 156

Baltimore, Maryland, 123–124
Baltimore Orioles, viii, 3–9, 17–19, 55–56, 145, 163–168, 169–176
Battey, Earl, 75
Bauer, Hank, 6, 7
Bavasi, Buzzy, 48
Becker, Joe, 46, 47, 50
Bell, Gus, 11
Berra, Yogi, 95–96, 158
Bluege, Ossie, 70
Boston Braves, 95
Boston Red Sox, 122, 140, 144
Bradenton, Florida, 102
Bragan, Bobby, 104, 108, 156
Brandt, Jackie, 39
Brooklyn, New York, 41–42, 57
Brooklyn Cadets, 149, 150–151
Brooklyn Dodgers, 41, 44–46, 148
Bruton, Bill, 114
Buhler, Bill, 38
Burdette, Lou, 147, 148

Cambria, Joe, 129, 131
Campanella, Roy, 158
Campanis, Al, 44–45
Cash, Norm, 122
Cepeda, Orlando, 81, 133
Charlotte (Twins' farm team), 132, 133
Chattanooga (Senators' farm team), 72
Chicago Cubs, 14, 23, 51
Chicago White Sox, 49, 140, 165
Cimoli, Gino, 164–165
Cincinnati, University of, 42
Cincinnati Reds, viii, 4, 6, 7, 9–17, 48, 105, 176

Clemente, Roberto, viii, 20–35
  in All-Star game, 23
  batting of, 22, 27–28
  childhood of, 24–25
  fielding of, 27
  injuries of, 28–32
  Most Valuable Player, 35
  photographs of, 20, 29, 34
  in Puerto Rico, 23–25
  in World Series, 22
Cleveland Indians, 19, 114, 145
Cobb, Ty, 134–135, 142
Cochrane, Mickey, 158
Columbia (Reds' farm team), 11
Crandall, Del, 152, 155
Cuba, viii, 129–131
Cy Young Award, 52

Dallas-Fort Worth (Twins' farm team), 135
Dalrymple, Clay, 80
Dalton, Harry, 9
Dark, Alvin, 84–85, 86–87, 88–90
Davis, Tommy, 95
Davis, Willie, 56
Dean, Dizzy, 49
Del Greco, Bobby, 80
Detroit Tigers, 111–114, 118–125, 171
DeWitt, William, 17–18
Dickey, Bill, 158, 168–169
DiMaggio, Joe, 108
Dodger Stadium, Los Angeles, 3, 51
Dominican Republic, viii, 81–83, 84–85, 91
Downs, Bunny, 98–99
Dressen, Charlie, 113, 152–153

INDEX

Drysdale, Don, 3–4, 5, 15, 19, 29, 37
Durocher, Leo, 103
Dykes, Jimmie, 11

Eastern League, 77
Eau Claire (Braves' farm team), 101, 152
Ebbets Field, Brooklyn, 44, 46

Feller, Bob, 49
Fenway Park, Boston, 6
Fernandena Beach, Florida, 131
Ford, Whitey, 86

Garagiola, Joe, 156, 161
Geraghty, Ben, 101–102, 153
Gilbert, Andy, 83
Golden Glove award, 164
Goryl, Johnny, 163–164
Griffith, Clark, 69–70
Griffith Stadium, Washington, 60–61
Groat, Dick, 22, *34*

Hamilton, Steve, 61
Harris, Bucky, *71*, 72, 113
Hartnett, Charles "Gabby", 158
Hitchcock, Billy, 156, 158
Houston Astros, 86, 87–88, 153
Howard, Elston, 120
Howser, Paul, 132
Hutchinson, Fred, 114

Indianapolis Clowns, 99–100

Jacksonville (Braves' farm team), 101, 108
Johnson, Blanche, 84
Johnson, Charlie, 123–124

Kaat, Jim, *141*
Kaline, Al, viii, 110–127
  batting of, 111, 113, 127
  childhood of, 123–124
  fielding of, 114, 127
  home runs of, 116
  injuries of, 117–122
  photographs of, *110, 115, 119, 121, 126*
  as team player, 114–117
Kansas City Athletics, 164
Kansas City Monarchs, 100
Kasko, Eddie, 13
Katalinas, Ed, 124
Killebrew, Harmon, viii, 58–75, 134
  batting of, 59–63, 65
  childhood of, 69–70
  home runs of, 59–62, 73
  injuries of, 66, 73
  photographs of, *58, 64, 67, 71, 74*
  as team player, 63–68, 75
  in World Series, 68

Koufax, Sandy, viii, 36–57, 104
  childhood of, 41–42
  Cy Young Award, 52
  injuries of, 37–41, 52, 54, 57
  Most Valuable Player, 52
  no-hitters of, 51
  perfect game of, 51
  photographs of, *36, 40, 43, 47, 53*
  pitching of, 38–39, 41, 46, 48, 50, 54–55
  strikeouts of, 49, 50, 51
  in World Series, 49, 52, 55–56, 68
Kuenn, Harvey, 38

INDEX

Landis, Jim, 165–166
Laurie, Milt, 42
Law, Vernon, 69, 104
Lefebvre, Jim, 38
Little Rock, Arkansas, 169
Los Angeles Angels, 137, 138
Los Angeles Dodgers, 3–4, 15, 19, 25–26, 29, 37–41, 48–57, 68, 95, 98, 103, 104, 105, 108, 175–176
Louisville (Braves' farm team), 152–153

Mantle, Mickey, 9, 26, 60, 61, 113, 117
Marichal, Gonzolo, 82
Marichal, Juan, viii, 76–91
   childhood of, 81–82
   in Dominican Republic, 81–83, 84–85, 91
   injuries of, 85, 86
   no-hitter of, 88
   photographs of, 76, 79, 89
   pitching of, 77–81, 87–90
   in World Series, 86
Mathews, Eddie, 13–14, 15, 147, 148
Mauch, Gene, 18
Mays, Willie, 23, 26–28, 60, 61, 90, 108, 113
McCovey, Willie "Stretch", 87–88
McHale, John, 124–125, 152, 156
McNally, Dave, 177
Mele, Sam, 62–65, 68, 73, 135, 142
Memorial Stadium, Baltimore, 4, 19
Miami Stadium, Miami, 6, 172

Michigan City (Giants' farm team), 77, 83
Midwest League, 77
Miller, Stu, 166
Milwaukee Braves, 13, 15, 25, 85, 88–90, 94–97, 100–108, 114, 147–150, 151–156
Mincher, Don, 65
Minnesota Twins, 59–60, 62–69, 75, 123, 129, 131, 163–164
Mitchell, Dale, 114
Mobile, Alabama, 97–99
Montreal (Dodgers' farm team), 26
Moon, Wally, 95
Mossi, Don, 172
Most Valuable Player award, 15, 22, 35, 52, 97, 174, 176
Muffet, Billy, 95
Mullen, John, 152
Murphy, Jimmy, 42, 44
Murtaugh, Danny, 30–31
Musial, Stan, 103

National League, 4, 9, 12, 15, 18, 21, 23, 35, 41, 46, 49, 86, 97, 103, 145, 155, 176
Negro American League, 99–100
New York Giants, 44
New York Mets, 51, 156
New York Yankees, 9, 22, 52, 61, 86, 97, 120, 166, 168
Newcombe, Don, 103
Northern League, 101, 152

Oakland, California, 9–10, 14

INDEX

Oliva, Tony, viii, 128–145
   batting of, 132–133, 137, 140–142
   childhood of, 130
   in Cuba, 129
   fielding of, 144–145
   injuries of, 138, 144
   photographs of, *128, 136, 139, 141, 143*
   Rookie of the Year, 138
Oliver, Gene, 106
Osinski, Dan, 138
Ott, Mel, 111–112, 125

Pacific Coast League, 78, 170
Palmer, Jim, 56
Pascual, Camilo, 144
Payette, Idaho, 69–70
Pepitone, Joe, 166
Perranoski, Ron, 19, 105
Pesky, Johnny, 72
Philadelphia Phillies, 13, 18, 33, 37–38, 49, 55, 78–81, 102, 124, 148
Phoenix, Arizona, 84–85
Piedmont League, 169
Pinson, Vada, 14
Pittsburgh Pirates, 21–24, 26–33, 54, 55, 69, 93–94, 104, 156
Pollock, Syd, 100
Pompez, Alex, 82–83
Post, Wally, 11
Powell, Boog, 166, 172
Power, Vic, 135
Powles, Gene, 10
Puerto Rico, viii, 22–25, 28, 32, 133, 138

Richardson, Bobby, *167*

Rigney, Bill, 78
Roberts, Robin, 13
Robinson, Brooks, viii, 4, 7, 162–178
   in All-Star game, 176
   batting of, 172–173, 174
   childhood of, 168–169
   fielding of, 163–166
   injuries of, 170–172
   Most Valuable Player, 174
   photographs of, *162, 167, 177*
   in World Series, 174–176
Robinson, Frank, vii-viii, 2–19, 175–176
   base running of, 7
   batting of, 6, 11, 19, 145
   childhood of, 9–10
   injuries of, 12, 15
   Most Valuable Player, 15
   photographs of, *2, 5, 8, 16*
   reckless play of, 12–14
   Rookie of the Year, 11
   Sophomore of the Year, 12
   traded, 4, 17–18
   Triple Crown, 9
   in World Series, 3–4, 19
Robinson, Jackie, 113
Rollins, Rich, 66
Rookie of the Year, 11, 138
Russell, Honey, 151–152
Ruth, Babe, 60, 62

Sain, Johnny, 145
St. Louis Cardinals, 23, 54, 95, 124
Sally League, 102
Salmon, Chico, 145

INDEX

San Francisco Giants, 30, 37, 44, 49, 54, 55, 77–81, 82–90, 94, 100, 108, 155
Scheffing, Bob, 113, 120
Schwarz, Jack, 82
Shaw, Bob, 49
Sherry, Norm, 49
Simmons, Curt, 102
Sisler, Dick, 17–18
Smith, Hal, 23
Sophomore of the Year, 12
Spahn, Warren, 23, 88–90, 147–148, 155, *159*
Sport Magazine, 113
Springfield (Giants' farm team), 77, 83
Sutherland, Gary, 37–38

Tacoma (Giants' farm team), 77
Taylor, Tony, 38, 80
Tebbetts, George "Birdie", 11, 156–158
Temple, Johnny, 153, *154*, 155
Terry, Ralph, 168
Texas League, 135
Thompson, Fresco, 44
Thomson, Bobby, 102
Tiger Stadium, Detroit, 120
Tighe, Jack, 113
Torre, Frank, 147–148, 161
Torre, Joe, viii, 146–161
   batting of, 153, 158
   catching of, 153–161
   childhood of, 147–149
   fielding of, 156
   home runs of, 158
   photographs of, *146, 154, 157, 159, 160*

Traynor, Pie, 176–177
Triple Crown, 9

Uecker, Bob, 39

Vancouver (Orioles' farm team), 170
Versalles, Zoilo, 134, 142

Walker, Harry, 31–35, 156
Walker, Rube, 44–45
Warwick, Carl, 88
Washington Senators, 60, 69–72, 140, 142
Weidner, Ed, 171
Weiss, George, 156
Welker, Senator Herman, 69–70
White, Bill, 38–39
Williams, Ted, 11, 134, 142
Wills, Maury, 39
Wine, Bobby, 39
Winston-Salem, North Carolina, 99
World Series games, 3–4, 19, 22, 23, 46, 49, 52, 54, 55–57, 68–69, 86, 95–97, 174–175, 176
Wytheville (Twins' farm team), 132, 144

Yankee Stadium, New York, 6, 7
Yastrzemski, Carl, 122
Yost, Eddie, 72

Zimmerman, Jerry, 145